glimmers of light in the darkness of life

existential reflections for everyday life

30 Devotional Studies from Ecclesiastes

trip kimball

WORD STRONG
WITH TRIP KIMBALL

copyrights

endorsements for glimmers of light in the darkness of life

If you are a true believer in Jesus Christ who wants to grow as one of His close followers, *Glimmers of Light in the Darkness of Life* can help you get there. If you are seeking the real meaning of life, this book will challenge your thinking and help you open your heart and mind to the truth. If you are hopeless, skeptical, or disillusioned by life as it seems to be, this book can elevate you from earth to heaven. God has a plan and has not run out of goodness, power, or wisdom to accomplish it.

— Pastor Bill Holdridge / Director of Poimen Ministries – https://www. poimenministries.com/

As a pastor, I've always found Ecclesiastes to be one of the hardest Bible books to read, understand or teach from. In *Glimmers of Light In the Darkness of Life*: Existential Reflections for Everyday Life, Trip Kimball has given a gift to pastors (and Christians) like me. He explores this enigmatic book in ways that are simple, practical, and profound. I highly recommend it!

— Pastor Karl Vaters / Pastor, Speaker, Podcaster, and Author – https:// karlvaters.com/

Trip and I worked together in the Philippines teaching Inductive Bible study. I always liked the way he thought and studied the Word. This book provides a solid and accessible study of Ecclesiastes. Any believer who wants help in answering some of life's tough questions will benefit from its truths. The structural format of commentary coupled with Inductive chapter study questions will be helpful for any small group discussion or individual study.

— Pastor Dan Finfrock / Director of Intensive Care Ministries – https://www.icmbible.com/

Glimmers of Light in the Darkness of Life, by Trip Kimball, is a wonderful, fresh, and practical read that deeply encourages the reader and was a delight for me to read! Trip's writing is clean, crisp, and clear under the anointing of the Holy Spirit. I loved this book!

— Dr. Chapin Marsh / President of Calvary Chapel University — https://calvarychapeluniversity.edu/

dedication

For my children — Jake, Becky, Pete, and Leanna and our grandchildren — Canaan, Bella, Berkeley, Eva, Brielle, Grace, and Ashford— may you—

Live clean, innocent lives as children of God,
shining like bright lights in a world full of crooked
and perverse people. Hold firmly to the word of
life; (Philippians 2:15-16 NLT)

And for those who struggle with the darkness of life in various ways—keep this in mind—

Those who are wise will shine like the brightness
on the horizon. Those who lead many people to
righteousness will shine like the stars forever and
ever. (Daniel 12:3 GW)

contents

foreword

From time to time, I'm asked to write a review for a book, or perhaps an endorsement. It's always an honor to be asked.

When author Trip Kimball asked me if I'd be willing to write something about *Glimmers of Light in the Darkness of Life*, I quickly consented—for two reasons: One reason has to do with the author. Trip Kimball has been a longtime friend, a brother I've known since 1987. But I don't write only as a friend, but also as a co-laborer with Trip in our mutual ministry of strengthening pastors (Poimen Ministries).

Prior to his involvement with Poimen Ministries, Trip faithfully and capably served for many years as a missionary in the Philippines, equipping pastors in inductive Bible study and sermon preparation. He also worked alongside his wife Susan in operating an amazing orphanage (Rainbow Village Ministries), a ministry God used to save many lives and add to God's kingdom. Trip also oversaw the Calvary Chapel Bible College and Training Center in Dumaguete City, Philippines, training Christian workers in God's Word. And before that, he planted and pastored a very fruitful church in Yucca Valley, CA called (at the time) Living Streams Christian Fellowship, now known as Joshua Springs Calvary Chapel.

The bottom line is that Trip is into discipleship, he's into training, he's into the church, and he's into compassion toward others. Hence, he's an ideal person to write a devotional commentary on the message of Ecclesiastes, an often misunderstood and misapplied book of the Bible.

This leads me to my second reason for writing this endorsement: Trip has done a tremendous job doing what he does best. He has brought our attention to what the text of Ecclesiastes says (observation), helped us identify what it means (interpretation), and finally, given us some very helpful keys for discovering how the Lord can use this important Old Testament book in our lives (application).

The format of *Glimmers of Light in the Darkness of Life* is easy to understand and use. If you are a true believer in Jesus Christ who wants to grow as one of His close followers, this book can help you get there. If you are seeking the real meaning of life, this book will challenge your thinking and help you open your heart and mind to the truth. If you are hopeless, skeptical, or disillusioned by life, as it seems to be, this book can elevate you from earth to heaven.

God has a plan and has not run out of goodness, power, or wisdom to accomplish it.

Today, the greatest need anywhere and everywhere is for people to read, study, and apply the Bible. The need is not to merely learn from the Bible, but to learn the Bible itself. The message of the Bible has the power to change a life, a family, a neighborhood, a city, a country, and the world.

If you're new to personal Bible study, *Glimmers of Light in the Darkness of Life* will help you dive into the Scriptures like never before.

Pastor Bill Holdridge

Director/ Poimen Ministries

preface

Here's an existential question many people ask—*Is life pointless or purposeful?*

If you are trying to make sense of life, this set of devotional studies from the book of Ecclesiastes offers simple but helpful answers to many of the tough questions in this *life under the sun*. Ecclesiastes is an enigmatic book of ancient wisdom that is often misunderstood and could be classified as *speculative wisdom*.[1] This is one book where it may be helpful to read the ending first before you dive in to study it.

The devotional studies in this book look at this ancient wisdom through the filter of the present, which shows how this wisdom applies to our lives today. Even though the wisdom found in Ecclesiastes is ancient, it's quite relevant for our present time. Cynicism and pessimism are common currents within western culture, and post-modern and nihilistic thought often skew our perspective on life and people. But as King Solomon observed and William Shakespeare echoed, there is "nothing new under the sun."

Perhaps nothing is new *under the sun*, but there are some glimmers of light in the darkness of life.

digging deeper

When you read Ecclesiastes the first time, I recommend doing it all in one sitting without stopping to think about things. This will help you keep the entire view and purpose of the book in mind. Also, take some time to read and consider what I wrote in the Prologue. It will help you understand what I mean by "existential reflections" compared to the philosophical sense of existentialism.

As you go back to read through Ecclesiastes at a slower pace, have a pencil or pen handy to mark your Bible, make some notes in the margin, and underline what stands out to you. Note the repetition of many phrases or thoughts. And while you're at it, keep a notebook or journal nearby to write your existential reflections. These are *my* existential reflections for everyday life from Ecclesiastes. I hope they will help you see some practical ways for applying what you learn in these devotional studies in your own daily life.

Following the devotionals for each chapter, you'll find study questions that will help you dig deeper into the text of Ecclesiastes. These study questions will guide you through the Bible text objectively and systematically based on the Inductive Bible Study (IBS) approach. Some questions ask for simple observations, others encourage more thought, and a few encourage you to make some practical applications of what you've read and studied. As a helpful resource, check out my *Introductory Guide to Inductive Bible Study*, along with a companion journal, *Living Word Study Journal*. You can find these on the "Shop" page of my website and my author page on Amazon.[2]

> **May God give you thoughtful reflections of your own to guide you in your life.**

author's note

Because the phrase occurs so often throughout Ecclesiastes, I've italicized the phrase—*(life) under the sun*—rather than put it in quotes each time. I want to emphasize this recurring theme without breaking sentences up with quotation marks.

I've used *GOD'S WORD* Translation (GW) for ease of reading, but for digital readers, the chapter text links on the *Study Questions* pages should take you to the text in a parallel version of GW and the NKJV text. Also, for further commentary, I recommend *Enduring Word* by Pastor David Guzik.[3]

As an Amazon Associate, I earn from qualifying purchases (books mentioned and linked).

prologue

Existential Reflections for Everyday Life from Ecclesiastes

The words of the spokesman, the son of David and the king in Jerusalem. "Absolutely pointless!" says the spokesman. "Absolutely pointless! Everything is pointless."(Ecclesiastes 1:1-2 GW)

---

is life pointless or purposeful?

I 've always questioned things. Perhaps I came to faith because I questioned what I heard and what I read. Growing up in a nominally Christian home, I jettisoned the religion of Christianity shortly after my confirmation classes in the Episcopal Church. This coincided with the social and political upheaval of the '60s and I jumped into that muddy river with both feet.

I took a comparative religions class in college, which I found interesting. Along with the assigned reading for the course, I also read the Bible each morning. Somehow, as I read through various religious texts, the person of Jesus kept surfacing in my mind. I read about and practiced meditation, and took part in other cultural practices of that era I'll leave unspecified, and felt compelled to read an old ASV (American Standard Version) Bible given to me by my beloved grandmother, who loved me with unconditional love. I understood little of what I read, but I kept reading that old Bible.

Still, I asked questions—lots of questions. And most of my questions went unanswered, as happens for many people, I guess. I asked basic existential questions like—Why are we here on this earth? What is the purpose of my life? Thankfully, I gained some spiritual direction during that tumultuous decade of the '60s. It pointed me to Jesus. And yet, many questions remained unresolved, as they are for many people today.

How do we not lose hope with so much evil, injustice, and uncertainty in the world? How does a person not become cynical or grow weary of life itself, when surrounded by such caustic and toxic social unrest and divisiveness?

The great King Solomon, once considered the wisest man in the world (1 Kings 4:29-31; 10:6-7), struggled with these same questions. They seemed to plague him in the later years of his life. Solomon's life was one of unparalleled success and indulgent excess. It was also a paradox of foolishness and wisdom because he didn't heed all of his own wise sayings, nor the warnings of the Lord and the Covenant Law of the Jewish people.

Many people who have read, or tried to read, through Ecclesiastes find it a difficult and discouraging book. It seems to pose more dilemmas and questions rather than provide any resolution or answers. But a careful and thoughtful reading of Ecclesiastes should help answer the question—

Is life pointless or purposeful?

some encouragement and guidance

When reading Ecclesiastes, we need to keep in mind an ancient world-view three thousand years removed from our present day. Solomon's observations, thoughts, and quandaries become difficult to wade through if you try to frame what's written in Ecclesiastes from a twenty-first-century viewpoint. It will make more sense when you view what Solomon says from how the world appeared in his day.

Ecclesiastes is one of five books collected as poetic wisdom books in the English canon of the Bible. Ecclesiastes is one of three books of wisdom, along with Job and Proverbs. In the Hebrew Bible, it is part of what is called the Ketuvim—the "Writings"—that includes several books after the books of the Law and Prophets.[1] It's written in an ancient form with a foil, where the answer to a seemingly unsolvable puzzle is revealed in the end. Solomon scatters glimpses of the conclusion throughout the book. I see these as *glimmers of light in the darkness of life*.

Ecclesiastes is the anglicized Greek word for the original word in Hebrew–Qohelet, which means "assembler." It's a term used to describe a teacher or preacher who calls people to assemble and speak wisdom to them. It could have several titles, such as—the *Preacher, Teacher, Spokesman* (as in GW), *Qohelet, Philosopher,* or the literal– *Leader of the assembly.*

Solomon repeats a few common words and phrases throughout the book, such as "under the sun," "trying to catch the wind," or "wisdom." Various Bible versions may use words and phrases differently, but the essence is the same. But by far, one word stands out the loudest and is repeated three times alone in verse 2—*pointless.* The Hebrew word is *hebel,* meaning "breath" or "vapor." It's translated into English Bible versions in several ways, such as *pointless, meaningless, vanity, futility,* and *useless.* This word is a metaphor for how fragile and temporary life seems. This is the undergirding theme of the entire book, and though stated at the end and the beginning, is not the last word (Ecclesiastes 1:2; 12:8).

Another way of saying it is — *"vapor, vapor… vapor of vapor"* — everything on earth and in life is just a vapor.

my existential reflections

The subtitle for this series of devotional studies is *Existential Reflections for Everyday Life*. These appear to be Solomon's philosophical reflections, made towards the end of his life, where he questions the value and purpose of all he did. This is not existential philosophy in an academic sense.[2] These are *my* existential reflections in response to Solomon's questions and quandaries about life. I see the book of Ecclesiastes as Solomon's existential reflections on *life under the sun*.

When I speak of existential reflections, I'm relating this to reflective thoughts about life, our existence, and our sense of being.[3] Existential philosophy is a modern philosophical approach to the meaning or value of life. Typically, many connect existential philosophy to nihilistic philosophers such as Albert Camus, Friedrich Nietzsche, or Jean-Paul Sartre, who saw no meaning or purpose in life. This is a generalization, but it lines up with what I learned in philosophy classes in college. There is a crucial difference between them and Soren Kierkegaard, a Danish theologian considered the first existentialist philosopher.[4] Kierkegaard was a genuine Christian believer and theologian, while Nietzsche was an avowed atheist and nihilist. Think beyond the stereotypical idea of existential philosophy when I use the phrase—*existential reflections*. My focus is on a more practical view of the essence of life rather than a philosophical one.

Throughout the book, you will see many contradictory thoughts and even some that don't fit the Christian theological narrative. There's a good reason for this. Solomon was viewing *life under the sun*. His view is earthbound, as it is for most people without the hope of resurrection. And yet, the Preacher speaks often of God (forty times) and even of the fear of the Lord (Ecclesiastes 3:14; 5:7; 7:18; 8:12; 12:13). So, keep this in mind as you read through these existential reflections of Solomon and know he is building up to an important exhortation at the end.

My hope is for these thoughts, questions, and statements to help you reflect on what I share in each devotional study and to see how they can apply to your life.

Do you struggle with certain questions about life?

Do you wonder about the purpose and value of your own life?

Do you wonder where God is in all the mess of life on earth?

If you answer "yes" to any, or all, of the questions above, read with an open mind and a prayerful heart.

a final thought...

Concerns about the environment, the future of the earth, social conflict and wars, and the safety and welfare of people all over the world cause concern for all of us. We're not in the Dark Ages, but it seems our world *is* getting darker.

What's our hope?

Our hope is in the only One *not* overcome by darkness (John 1:5 NIV). The very One who spoke light into existence (Genesis 1:3).

Trusting in God gives us *glimmers of light in the darkness of life.*

1 /
is there really anything new under the sun?

Whatever has happened before will happen again. Whatever has been done before will be done again. There is nothing new under the sun. Can you say that anything is new? It has already been here long before us. (Ecclesiastes 1:9-10 GW)

[context– Ecclesiastes 1:3-11 GW]

the elusive pursuit of happiness

My wife and I grew up in what has become a wealthy beach area in Southern California. Soon after we started our own family, we moved inland to the high desert where I planted a church. Settled into a comfortable way of life and fruitful ministry, God began showing us a different plan for our lives beyond our expectations. After twelve years of ministry, we moved eight thousand miles overseas to the Philippines. God led us to begin two thriving and fruitful ministries in the fifteen years we lived overseas.

Then we moved back to our home culture of America. We moved to northeastern Florida where our sons lived, but where we had no personal friends. We also took on the responsibility of caring for my ailing dad. And we endured the usual reentry shock most missionaries experience when coming *home*. But it was a very different new home for us. Our lives changed in drastic ways as we navigated reentry and caring for my dad.

Our biggest concern was to not get swept up by the torrent of consumerism in American culture. As a nation, we Americans thrive on what's new. Newness—the latest and greatest—seems to be the engine of our economy, and the goal of our pursuit of happiness. Businesses and social media networks push people toward this elusive pursuit. Don't commercials tout the latest and greatest clothing style, car, or big meal deal that we *must* go out and buy? I mean... *how can we live* without such things?

We bought an older house in the beach area of our city. When we first moved back to the US, I would take the five-block walk to the beach or walk around our house in amazement at all we had. Because it's an older house, we needed to update and upgrade several things like windows, siding, and our roof. These were big-ticket items but needed improvements. Although we had legitimate needs to address in our home, it led us to watch way too many home improvement shows on TV and peruse the latest DIY magazines. But soon, as we began doing projects on the house, I imagined even more possibilities of remodeling we could do. It was a slippery slope! I had to catch myself from falling into the bottomless pit of "home improvement" and return to being thankful for all we had already.

With all we have, shouldn't we be happy? I guess so. Yet, we know people in America are often *unhappy*. We see more and more people seek medication for depression and anxiety. Our collective pursuit of happiness is an elusive, never-ending effort. This leaves many people feeling empty.

Like vultures, the news networks go after the latest tragedy, disaster, or terrorist attack, then flood us with repeated images and sound bites. The inundation we receive from the news media and social media overwhelms us—leaving us numb and empty inside. And yet, this is nothing new. Ancient wisdom tells us this. Could it be we are looking for the wrong kind of happiness, in the wrong places, and in the wrong way? This is the point, more or less, of the book of Ecclesiastes.

insights

King Solomon amassed great wealth, had hundreds of wives and concubines, and was well-educated, yet he viewed it all as pointless. What would bring him to that view of life? Well, that's a long story, but it leads to the wisdom found in Ecclesiastes. Ecclesiastes is written in an ancient philosophical form called speculative wisdom.[1] General philosophical questions about human existence, suffering, or humanity in relation to God characterize this type of wisdom. These questions go beyond rational abstract thought and make it speculative wisdom.[2]

Solomon often uses figurative language to contrast worldliness with godly wisdom. Figurative language is used to illustrate or relate a thought or concept that is not familiar or easily understood to something familiar in a physical sense. For example, Solomon spoke of the transitory nature of generations on earth with the constancy of the earth itself. He speaks of the continuing cycles of the sun rising and setting, the directions of the wind, and the flow of rain, streams, and the ocean as endless cycles. These are his examples of the pointlessness of life.

> *"Absolutely pointless!" says the spokesman. "Absolutely pointless! Everything is pointless." (Ecclesiastes 1:2 GW)*

Solomon speaks of the redundancy of life itself.

All we do in life, no matter how new or special it may seem, has been done before. Solomon drives home this cynical view of life by returning to various generations of people that come and go and then forgotten. Perhaps our lack of awareness or remembrance of past events and stories of former generations is a reason we don't seem to learn from history. Later generations lose perspective or can't relate to even cataclysmic events from history. We try to keep what's historically significant alive through holidays and events set aside to remind us of them, but after a few generations, even these lose their impact on younger generations wrapped up in current events and concerns.

existential reflections for everyday life

We are creatures of habit. Some of us maintain a daily routine or schedule. Others don't appear to have a rigid or set schedule yet still have a pattern of doing the same things day in and day out. We need some kind of order in our lives and in the world. No one does well with chaos. Chaotic and jumbled thoughts and actions could be indicators of mental illness or a serious physical condition. However, unbroken routines can become monotonous. They dull our creativity, energy, and resolve. So we need to take breaks and enjoy recreation and vacations.

When it comes to the broader view of the meaning and purpose of our lives and how we fit in the greater scheme of the world and universe, well, it's complicated. Our worldview—how we view the world and our place in it all—is a very personal and subjective issue. What makes it complicated is our individuality. We are distinct and unique from others. And yet, the basis for how we view the world simplifies it all.

Our worldview affects our sense of meaning and purpose in life. This is the crux of the book of Ecclesiastes. When our worldview is earthbound and based on human nature, it's easy to develop a cynical or pessimistic worldview.

What is your worldview based on?

Do you see life on earth as boring and pointless or as having meaning and purpose?

A true and positive worldview helps us rise above the cynical and pessimistic view so often presented by those who don't believe or trust in God.

When we believe God is the Creator and Lord of all, we are more likely to see an order and purpose in our life.

2 /
if knowledge is power, can ignorance be bliss?

I've used my mind to understand wisdom and knowledge as well as madness and stupidity. Now I know that this is like trying to catch the wind. With a lot of wisdom comes a lot of heartache. The greater your knowledge, the greater your pain. (Ecclesiastes 1:17-18 GW)

[context– Ecclesiastes 1:12-18 GW]

trying to catch the wind

If we knew all that would happen to us in our lifetime, it would either paralyze us with fear or motivate us to make different decisions. Several movies and stories have alternative endings where someone goes back in time to change an event or decision. They try to change the outcome of their life. But life isn't a series of events. It's much more. How can you or I list all the people and experiences of our life? As said many times before, a person's life is more than the dash between their birthdate and the date of their death on a grave marker.

One of my favorite things about having grandchildren is watching them learn and grow from infancy to adulthood. We don't always appreciate this enough while raising our own children because life is busy. As grandparents, we often enjoy the wonder and surprise seen in our grandchildren's eyes as they discover some new thing, taste, or experience in life. We delight in their newfound knowledge of things we already know. We reflect upon the wonderment and innocence of childhood that we lose as we grow older.

Solomon's thoughts and words in Ecclesiastes—his existential reflections—reveal the way *knowledge is power* and *ignorance is bliss* converge as a conundrum. His pursuit of more knowledge, both experientially and philosophically, brought "a lot of heartache" and was "like trying to catch the wind." This brings to mind the astounding amounts of time we spend on social media in our voyeuristic pursuit of trivial knowledge.

The catchphrase, "knowledge is power," became popular in the age of Information Tech (IT). We usually attribute this expression to Sir Francis Bacon, a philosopher, statesman, and scientist.[1] Considered the originator of the scientific method, when he spoke of knowledge being power, he spoke of science as we think of it today.[2] Currently, we link the expression *knowledge is power* to the abundance of information available via the internet. But information doesn't always produce knowledge. The conflicting and confusing information available on the internet today makes this self-evident. The concept of knowledge as power has more ancient roots than in the sixteenth century (Bacon). This same thought is in the book of Proverbs, where knowledge is related to wisdom rather than mere information (Proverbs 24:5-6 GW).

The opposite end of this spectrum is the expression "ignorance is bliss."[3] If this seems contradictory to *knowledge is power*, it is. And yet, there is some merit to the idea of ignorance as bliss. After a lifetime of pursuing wisdom and knowledge, Solomon says it's "like trying to catch the wind." Is he implying that ignorance is bliss? Can ignorance really be bliss?

insights

Solomon refers to himself as the king of Jerusalem, as if to verify the gravity of his thoughts about life. Some commentaries question whether Solomon is the actual author of Ecclesiastes, but much of its content seems unique to him. No other king of Jerusalem could say such things.

A repeated theme in this book is the burden of trying to make sense of all that takes place in life *under the sun*. This fourth exclamation emphasizes how futile this search is. Solomon uses a phrase repeated throughout the book to underscore how pointless the effort is to understand life. He says it's "like trying to catch the wind." Solomon then describes the limitations upon us all—

> No one can straighten what is bent. No one can count
> what is not there. (Ecclesiastes 1:15 GW)

These are Solomon's inner struggles. He says, "I thought to myself...," as he reflects on his personal investment in wisdom and knowledge. He concludes—we only gain great heartache and pain by seeking more and more wisdom and knowledge. The conclusion of chapter 1 is a warning Solomon unpacks in later thoughts.

existential reflections for everyday life

What can we do with all this negative and discouraging talk? The way to keep from becoming cynical and hardened in our hearts is to maintain a sense of perspective. We need to have a hope greater than our thoughts and experiences. We need to hold on to what we know instead of becoming weighed down with the burden of what we can't change or understand. This requires some existential reflection of our own.

I grew up in a dysfunctional family, as many of us did. Our family had a multi-generational legacy of alcoholism, addiction, and infidelity. By high school, I was well on my way to carrying on this questionable legacy. But a devastating breakup with a long-time girlfriend became a catalyst to interrupt my part of the legacy. I remember a sense of sheer aching hollowness like a great void inside my soul. I felt helpless and hopeless and empty with this great void inside, adrift in life without this relationship.

This incident intersected with a spiritual quest in my life. I was on a quest to know God. Did He exist? I wanted to know Him—if indeed He was knowable. Little by little, I regained some direction and perspective. I started reading a Bible that someone gave me, going to church, and praying. In fact, praying became a simple source of relief and peace for me. I had so many questions but few answers. The more I struggled with what I didn't know, the more confused I became. At some point, God intervened in this struggle during my Bible reading and clarified *why* I was struggling. I needed to hold on to what I *could* understand and trust what I didn't to Him.

We can't "straighten what is bent" as if it were never bent. And we can't "count what is not there." We can't know what we don't know. Every person has limitations. This is the reality of being human. God is sovereign and knows all things. He alone can restore or straighten what is bent, including you and me. He is the One who hung the stars in the universe and even named them, yet we cannot see or count them all (Isaiah 40:25-26 GW). Genuine faith isn't a set of beliefs and values we hold. Faith is an implicit trust in God.[4] We trust in His existence and He promises to honor and reward our trust in Him (Hebrews 11:6).

When we see futility and senselessness in life, we need to remember— our lives, all lives, have purpose and meaning. Challenged with what we don't understand, we need to entrust such dilemmas to the Lord, who *does* understand. When our sense of who we are is centered and grounded on the Lord, we gain an eternal perspective. We have a hope that surpasses everything life on earth offers.

Is your life grounded and centered on the Lord, or are you still trying to catch the wind?

Do you have faith to see beyond what your limitations are?

God can straighten what is bent. He knows what you don't know. God is able to restore and fulfill a sense of purpose and significance in your life.

When your life seems adrift—ask God to help you and trust Him to do so.

study questions for ecclesiastes chapter 1

For a more thorough study, read through Ecclesiastes Chapter 1 again to consider and answer the following questions—

1. What are the main thoughts of the first eleven verses?
2. What is the main reason for "the spokesman" saying these things, as made clear in verses 12-18?
3. Have you had similar thoughts to these? If so, why?
4. What does this spokesman (King Solomon) say about gaining all of his wisdom?
5. Do you ever feel life is pointless? If so, what brings you to that place?
6. What makes you happy? What is most important in your life?
7. What are ways you find to break the routine of life?
8. How do you keep a positive view of life when it seems monotonous and pointless?

3 /
the problem with me, myself, and the pursuit of pleasure

I thought to myself, "Now I want to experiment with pleasure and enjoy myself." But even this was pointless. I thought, "Laughter doesn't make any sense. What does pleasure accomplish?" (Ecclesiastes 2:1-2 GW)

[context– Ecclesiastes 2:1-11 GW]

it's never enough

Because I have a US passport and the means to travel, I have done so far more than the pastors I worked alongside for over thirty years in the Philippines and other countries. God gave me the opportunity to travel to many places in the world to serve Him as a missionary. Each country I visit reminds me of how blessed and privileged I am as an American. The cost of one person going on a short-term mission is equivalent to or greater than one national pastor's annual salary in most other nations. This helps me keep a healthy perspective.

It can puff me up with pride or humble me. Sadly, it's done both. When I cross the line between privilege and pride, I know I need to humble myself. I need this awareness to keep my foolish pride in check. Working alongside national pastors in various nations, I wonder how I would do in their circumstances. Would I be content to serve as they do? Would I be as faithful as them?

In America, we live like millionaires. I don't have a million dollars, nor do I expect to become a millionaire, but compared to most of the world's population, the average American lives like a millionaire. Unless you've traveled to under-developed nations—what I call MOTROW (*most of the rest of the world*)—it may seem hard to accept that you live like a millionaire.[1] But sixty years ago, flight travel was uncommon for most Americans. Not anymore. Looking back to the fifties, the average home was smaller, and people had fewer possessions. As a nation, we have more wealth per capita now than ever, yet it's still not enough for many of us.

> **Here's the problem with pleasure and wealth.**
> **It's never enough.**

This is one reason I value Solomon's wisdom and why I need to learn from his failures and weaknesses. King Solomon, who was beyond wealthy and able to pursue as much pleasure as he wanted, realized the problem with pleasure and getting everything you want.

Many people fantasize about what it would be like to be rich and powerful. We see this by who we venerate in our culture. Athletes and entertainers make outrageous amounts of money and live at a level we can only imagine. CEOs receive huge salaries and bonuses and act as if they deserve them even when their companies lose money. Even within the church, many pastors and leaders of ministries receive well-above-average salaries, as their mega-churches claim to build bigger and better buildings for the kingdom. This tells me we have learned little from the wisest and wealthiest king of Israel.

insights

In these opening verses of chapter two, at least three things stand out to me. Solomon uses an abundance of personal pronouns—me, myself, and I. This reveals a pursuit of pleasure without the restraint of conscience. These verses reveal someone who was self-absorbed. What I call the "me, myself, and I syndrome" plagued King Solomon. Of course, this is common to American culture today, just as prominent among younger generations as it was during the '70s in the "Me Generation."[2] But it's an ancient problem.

Solomon says he intentionally pursued a pleasure-filled life, and this included enjoying wine to a point of excess. He tried to live without restraint and tested the boundaries of excess because he could. He justified living without restraint as his "reward for all my hard work" (Ecclesiastes 2:10 GW). What work did Solomon do? Here's a shortlist—

> *I accomplished some great things: I built houses for myself.*
> *I planted vineyards for myself. I made gardens and*
> *parks for myself. I planted every kind of fruit tree in*
> *them. I made pools to water the forest of growing trees.*
> *I bought male and female slaves. In addition, slaves were*
> *born in my household. I owned more herds and flocks*
> *than anyone in Jerusalem before me.*
> *I also gathered silver and gold for myself. I gathered the*
> *treasures of kings and provinces. I provided myself*
> *with male and female singers and the pleasures men*
> *have with one concubine after another. (Ecclesiastes*
> *2:4-8 GW).*

"I" precedes each of Solomon's accomplishments. Though these accomplishments may seem desirable, they weren't honorable in God's eyes, and God judged him accordingly (1 Kings 11:6, 9 GW). And yet, his conscience was ever-present throughout his plunge into pleasure, which led him to realize how his selfish pursuit of pleasure was *"pointless... like trying to catch the wind. I gained nothing."* (Eccl 2:3, 9, 11 GW).

When Solomon speaks of his wisdom remaining with him throughout his pursuits, he's referring to his conscience. This serves as an example of how we can suppress our conscience and become numb to it. Our conscience is our God-implanted sense of right and wrong. It's what C. S. Lewis called *the Moral Law* in his book, *The Case for Christianity*.[3]

Solomon's life proves it is dangerous to ignore our conscience.

existential reflections for everyday life

As I reflect on all of this, it brings to mind both a question and a certainty. How far is too far and beyond the reach of God's grace? Once we step over a line, we can't go back to the way things were. Whatever boundary we cross, whether good or bad, we can't cross back over it as if we'd never stepped over that boundary.

We have free will to make choices, but every choice has a consequence. Some choices are excellent and have favorable consequences, like treating others with kindness or exercising self-control. Other choices are harmful and lead us to destructive consequences, such as lying, hurtful words, or carelessness. Once we tell a lie, we need to continue the first lie with more lies or tell the truth. But just like hurtful words, we can't take back the lie, just as we can't take back hurtful words.

This is where our conscience is so important.

When our conscience is grounded in the truth and wisdom of God, we are more likely to listen and heed its subtle warnings. What if our conscience warns us to not cross a certain line but we do so anyway? Eventually, the question comes up—How far is too far beyond the reach of God's grace? The simple answer is that even where sin is abundant, God's grace is greater and more abundant (Romans 5:20). Several current-day testimonies affirm this, as does Paul the apostle's life (1 Corinthians 15:9-10).

One of the most powerful testimonies of this is Pastor John Newton's life.[4] He is the author of the beloved hymn, *Amazing Grace*. John

Newton began as a captain of a slave-trading ship and became known as the Great Blasphemer. Though raised in the Christian faith, he led a vile, shameful life until his conversion. God restored him after he repented during a terrible storm and later became an influential pastor in England. But there's so much more to his life story and why he wrote Amazing Grace,[5] you need to read it for yourself.[6]

Newton's life is an example of crossing a line with great consequences and experiencing the powerful restoration of God's grace. Once we cross a moral line, we can't go back to how things were before, but we can go forward by God's grace. When a person tries to rationalize or deny their experiences in life, it is a futile effort. We cannot escape the age-old law of sowing and reaping. Choices have consequences. Good choices have beneficial consequences, but foolish choices have detrimental consequences.

This is the reality Solomon expresses in the opening verses of chapter 2. He's done it all and realized it wasn't worth it. The unspoken thought is this—surely there is more to this life than wealth and pleasure. If you keep reading through Ecclesiastes, you'll see how Solomon answers this question and others. Learn from Solomon's example of what *not* to do.

If you cross lines you shouldn't, ask the Lord to restore you by His grace and guide you by His Spirit to help you make better choices.

our life's legacy ought to be a gift from god to others

Then I turned my attention to experience wisdom, madness, and foolishness. For instance, what can the man who replaces the king do? Only what has already been done. But I saw that wisdom has an advantage over foolishness as light has an advantage over darkness. (Ecclesiastes 2:12-13 GW)

There is nothing better for people to do than to eat, drink, and find satisfaction in their work. I saw that even this comes from the hand of God....God gives wisdom, knowledge, and joy to anyone who pleases him. But to the person who continues to sin, he gives the job of gathering and collecting wealth. The sinner must turn his wealth over to the person who pleases God. Even this is pointless. It's like trying to catch the wind. (Ecclesiastes 2:24-26 GW) [context– Ecclesiastes 2:12-26 GW]

perception and perspective

In my early forties, my family and I moved eight thousand miles overseas, but without our oldest son. We gave him the option to move with us or to finish his final year of high school at home. He stayed to work toward academic scholarships for his college education. We honored his decision, but that first year of separation as a family was hard on all of us. This was an important and good decision, but it brought criticism from others. One of my wife's friends asked her how she could leave her firstborn son and move halfway across the world. At first, this hurt her deeply, but God comforted her. He reminded Susan that as a Father—He had sent His own Son into the world as an infant to be the Savior of the world.

Over the years, my wife and I were partners in many ministries. We invested much time, energy, and love in these endeavors and in people. We worked hard to establish these ministries, especially in the beginning. As the Lord led us on to new ways to serve Him, we had to let go of what was and embrace what was yet to be. This often involved some type of personal loss and sadness. Most of these changes were beyond our control. Some were because of the choices we made. In our fifteen years overseas, we cared for many babies, children, and abused girls. They all had heartbreaking stories. We endured several tragedies, including a devastating fire that took the lives of five children.[1] Although there were many tough times, we saw God bring redemption to so many lives. Seeing many lives restored helped us maintain a sense of perspective. Our faith and trust in God made it possible to endure these challenges. We saw beyond what appeared impossible through the light of hope and trust in the Lord.

We saw beyond our doubts and disappointments by faith.

Our perception, how we understand life around us, our perspective and our outlook on life are important. How do we understand life around us? What is our outlook on it all? When a time of darkness seems to descend upon us, how do we perceive it and navigate it? When we are shortsighted and see only the darkness of our immediate situation, all may seem lost. This is the perception King Solomon had about his own life's work. But if we see other possibilities beyond our immediate circumstances, it changes everything. This is why faith is so important (see Hebrews 11:6 GW).

insights

As King Solomon continued to explore life to a point of excess—to experience wisdom, madness, and foolishness—he came to two conclusions. First, wisdom is better than foolishness, just as light is better than darkness. Solomon explained the advantage of one over the other. A wise person observes what he sees and walks in the light of his understanding. But a fool is oblivious to what is around him. He lacks understanding and walks in his own darkness.

Solomon's second realization is about his legacy. Solomon was concerned about who would succeed him as king and inherit all he worked hard to accomplish. History reveals there was a good reason for his concern. After Solomon's death, his son Rehoboam succeeded him as king of Israel, but he didn't have his father's wisdom. Because of Rehoboam's heavy-handed tactics, the kingdom of Israel divided and never returned to the glory it knew under David and Solomon (2 Chronicles 9:31; 11:2-4). Solomon realized his legacy—what he had accomplished in life—would end when he died. So it seemed to him there was no difference between his death and the death of a fool who lived in the darkness of his ignorance. This concern is a continuing theme in Ecclesiastes, but it is not the last word on the subject, nor the conclusion Solomon makes in the end.

Reading the end of Ecclesiastes chapter two, it would be easy to get lulled back into Solomon's cynical view of life. He ends the chapter with his oft-repeated theme of how pointless life is *under the sun*. But the last few verses of this chapter hold a surprise. Solomon gives a reason to find satisfaction in life through our work. He also gives a slightly optimistic perception of what we see as a legacy, but he gives it in a broader sense than for one person. As in Solomon's Proverbs, we see a generalized perspective on what we leave behind after death.

Let's consider what Solomon sees as a reason to be encouraged. At first, it may sound like a concession. It's as if Solomon hates to admit there's a way to be content with one's life and work. He says, *"There is nothing better for people to do than to eat, drink, and find satisfaction in their work."* But this is more than a consolation prize. It is *"... from the hand of God."* It's a gift from God. Solomon doubles down on this thought when he says, *"Who can eat or enjoy themselves without God?"*

Of course, it's easy to view work as drudgery, but God created us for work. The first humans had a great responsibility to oversee the paradise God created. God created woman as man's partner for this work (Genesis 1:26-30; 2:18-23). The curse came because they disobeyed God's command not to eat from one specific tree. God didn't pronounce a curse on work itself, but He pronounced it on the ground where the man would do his work (Genesis 3:17-19). Work gives us a sense of purpose. It gives us an opportunity to be productive partners on earth.

Solomon sees a more redemptive view of work than many of us might have. He expands on this more in later chapters, but here Solomon says people should see work as a gift from God and to *"... find satisfaction in their work."* In the next verse, we see a promise hidden in these encouraging thoughts—

> *God gives wisdom, knowledge, and joy to anyone who*
> *pleases him (Ecclesiastes 2:26a GW).*

Solomon based this promise on a simple trust in God. And yet, we see the contrast to *not* trusting in God in the continuation of the same verse—

> *But to the person who continues to sin, he gives the job of*
> *gathering and collecting wealth. The sinner must turn*
> *his wealth over to the person who pleases God.*

These few verses at the end of chapter two remind us of our responsibility to choose how we perceive things. We can view work as drudgery or as an opportunity. Since God made us in His image, our work is a partnership with God in His creation. When we trust in God, we can also see it as a gift when we find satisfaction in our work. As Solomon said, *"this comes from the hand of God."*

In what way do you see your life and work?

existential reflections for everyday life

The desire to leave a legacy lasting beyond our death is something we all grapple with, and too often, we equate a person's legacy with their estate and life accomplishments. This is the shortsighted view of Solomon in the second chapter of Ecclesiastes.

If all we leave behind is some wealth or property or accomplishments —no matter how significant they are in the sight of others—it's easy to feel disillusioned about the end of life. But we don't need to be so shortsighted. There are countless examples of squandered family legacies scattered throughout history. Family businesses passed on to children often fail. Heirs waste fortunes with extravagant and foolish lifestyles. Even important accomplishments or discoveries may only last for a few decades, perhaps just a few years.

Consider what or who is most important to you. What has eternal or lasting value to you? We can discover what King Solomon says about this later, but this is a personal concern for each of us. I can only share my thoughts about this. I can't answer these questions for you, nor can anyone else.

My family is my most valuable living legacy on earth. People I've had the privilege to lead, disciple, and serve are the next most important and valuable legacy for me. I believe the only accomplishments that have true value are those that are an investment in the lives of others within God's Kingdom. That kind of investment is invaluable when it leads people to trust in God. It continues beyond our brief lives into eternity. It has eternal value. This type of legacy lives beyond the moment of our life within eternity and extends beyond whatever we may think is our destiny.

What value will your life have beyond the grave?

What do you think your legacy will be beyond death?

With your perception and perspective grounded in the Lord, you can see beyond difficulties and obstacles by faith.

You can also be confident in the value of your life's legacy when you look through the lens of faith—a genuine trust in God.

study questions for ecclesiastes chapter 2

For a more thorough study, read through Ecclesiastes Chapter 2 again to consider and answer the following questions broken into 2 sections—

Questions for Chapter 2:1-11—

1. What is the spokesman's (Solomon's) intended pursuit?
2. What was his conclusion after this pursuit?
3. What does Solomon say was a constant guide to him? How was it helpful?
4. What are the things Solomon did and what did he gain in his pursuit of pleasure?
5. What was his (Solomon's) realization, and what helped him arrive at it?
6. Do you secretly (or not so secretly) wish you could win the lottery, or get rich some other way?
7. What are the things you daydream or fantasize about?
8. Do you envy or resent people whose lives seem better than yours? Or do you envy and resent them?
9. What do you think is key to being content with the life you have now?

For Chapter 2:12-26—

1. What life situation causes King Solomon to view life as pointless?
2. Why does he come to this conclusion, and how does this affect his outlook on life?
3. What does Solomon realize after thinking of all of these things?
4. How does this realization bring a better perspective and value to life itself?
5. What things cause you to lose sight of the value of life?
6. What (or who) is most important in your life? Does this help you see beyond yourself, or make you more self-focused?
7. When you acknowledge God's existence, how does this help you have a better outlook on life?
8. What are specific ways for you to view life beyond yourself?

the cycles and seasons of life under the sun

Everything has its own time, and there is a specific time for every activity under heaven: (Ecclesiastes 3:1 GW)

To everything there is a season, a time for every purpose under heaven: (Ecclesiastes 3:1 NKJV)

[context– Ecclesiastes 3:1-8 GW]

---

history is beyond our control

Looking back on my life, it's easy to see my childhood and adolescence weren't unique. I grew up in a typical middle-class American family. We lived in an area full of wealthy families, but our life wasn't so different. Sure, the lifestyle many of my friends enjoyed was beyond our reach economically, but their home life was similar. I realized this while spending time in my friends' homes and observing their family life, or lack of it. Alcoholism and infidelity were common and often resulted in divorce, but my parents stayed married despite our family's dysfunctional state.

As my wife and I came to faith and started our own family, we chose a different path than our parents. Our involvement in full-time ministry was a huge departure from what most of our childhood friends pursued. Still, we faced the same challenges any family would face raising four children. Our marriage went through some rocky seasons, but we remained committed in our vows to one another. Even our ministry life went through seasons of change.

Just as history goes through various cycles, so do we. Solomon wrote about these seasons of life *under the sun* in Ecclesiastes. As said in his famous quote—*Is there anything new under the sun?*[1] The world we grew up in changed drastically from the turmoil of the sixties to the intrusion of terrorism at the beginning of the twenty-first century. But these are just the cyclic rhythms of world history seen throughout centuries and millennia.

History may repeat itself, but we cannot control it.

We also can't erase history, although many have attempted to do so. The attempt to rewrite history is a way of trying to control people's beliefs, thoughts, and behavior. As time passes, efforts to change history to fit a certain set of beliefs will be exposed. This illustrates the great and continuing struggle between the will of humanity and the sovereignty of God. All these attempts to control or revise history fail because God is greater than any generation, philosophy, political movement, or religion.

There are many examples of the ultimate failure of attempts to control people through a forced ideology and the accompanying efforts to revise history to support that ideology. The emperor of Babylon, Nebuchadnezzar, tried to reeducate some bright young Jewish men taken captive from Judah in Israel. He gave Daniel and three of his cohorts Babylonian names and put them through a strict regimen and indoctrination. But these young men resisted in ways that allowed them to maintain their identity and faithfulness to their God (Daniel 1:8-16). The ideologies of Nazism and Communism gained powerful control over many people for a time. This attempt to control ultimately failed to subvert people's beliefs and yearning for freedom.

These examples illustrate how people attempt to control and reshape the future.

The first attempt to gain this type of control was in the Garden of Eden when the first man and woman believed the lie of the serpent (Genesis 3:4-5). Several generations later, with humanity united in one place with one language, they attempted to build an observation tower up to the heavens on the plain of Shinar, later known as Babylon. They desired to build a great city and tower to become famous and keep from being scattered throughout the earth. But God saw the danger of this effort to control their own destiny and the destiny of humanity. God confused their language and scattered people throughout the earth with many languages (Genesis 11:1-9).

Why would God do this? Humanity's attempt to be sovereign over themselves and others is based on the prideful attempt to gain ultimate control over life on earth. But God had greater plans. Much greater. He wanted to restore humanity to the true freedom the first man and woman knew *before* the serpent's lie.

insights

Life on earth—*under the sun*—is full of cycles and seasons. We see this in the natural world—the annual seasons of weather, a myriad of ecological cycles, and the rhythm of everyday life. This is what Solomon expressed in his list of alternating contrasts (*see the full text on the coming page entitled—"Scripture Text"*). It's a reminder of humanity's limited capacity to control our lives *under the sun*. God is sovereign, but we are not. He reigns over the earth, the heavens, and all life.

King Solomon observed the ongoing rhythms of life on earth and concluded life is not random—it has a cyclical order and purpose. We may struggle to see the purpose of these seasons of life because we're in the midst of them. Even over the course of a lifetime, we may find it difficult to understand why some things take place or if they have any value or purpose.

When we look at things from God's perspective—an eternal view—we can begin to understand. But *how* do we do this? The Scriptures reveal valuable life lessons, practical instruction, and wisdom in their many narratives. In particular, the Gospels reveal who God is and His plan and purpose of redemption for all humanity. Reading God's written Word helps us to see life from God's perspective.

We also need to spend time with godly people who have valuable life experiences. All of us need encouragement and can be encouragers to others. We all benefit from people who are mentors in our life — not only older, more experienced people, but fellow travelers in life's journey. I've benefited from mentors who were older and more experienced than me, and I've also benefited from my peers who saw things differently from me. I've learned things through people who've served with me in ministry and even from my children. My wife, who is my faithful ministry and life partner, often helps me see people and situations much more clearly than I do.

Looking at Solomon's list of life events, it's easy to see the contrasts. Of course, these great pendulum swings of life's events are not so easy to endure. But these contrasting actions and life events reveal the cyclical nature of life on earth. We may not go through each of these in our own lives, but may know others who have, or observed others who have. It's important to view this list of actions and life events from the culture and time of King Solomon, but many of them are relatable to all people in any era.

existential reflections for everyday life

Solomon's key point is this—there's a purpose for all that takes place in life. We may not understand the purpose in our own life or the lives of others, but God knows, for they are *His* purposes. The point isn't to understand what the purpose is and why an event happens. It is to realize and understand it's not random, nor is it fate. I'm always wary of anyone who is quick to say they know why some cataclysmic or tragic event took place as if they know God's will and purposes.

Life is not random nor is it predetermined or fixed.

Our family went through a tragic event many years ago. As most people do, I found myself asking God, "Why did this happen?" I still may not understand the reason all these years later, but I don't need to know it. My wife and I trusted God during this tragedy and the long recovery from it. We saw God do many amazing things in our lives and in the lives of the people we served alongside in the ministry we led. (You can read more about it here—Out of the Ashes).[2] We don't need to understand why some events beyond our control occur. But we need to understand it is neither random nor fate. When we entrust our life and those we love to the Lord, we need to continue trusting in Him beyond what we do or do not understand.

What are you going through in your life today?

Do you recognize a cycle or season from this list that resonates with you now?

What do you need to entrust to God today?

There is a purpose for every season and cycle in life.

[The text for Ecclesiastes 3:1-8 in two Bible versions is on the following pages.]

scripture text

Comparison of Ecclesiastes 3:1-8 (GW
and NKJV)

———

Ecclesiastes 3:1-8 (GW)

*Everything has its own time, and there is a specific time
    for every activity under heaven:
a time to be born and a time to die,
a time to plant and a time to pull out what was planted,
a time to kill and a time to heal,
a time to tear down and a time to build up,
a time to cry and a time to laugh,
a time to mourn and a time to dance,
a time to scatter stones and a time to gather them,
a time to hug and a time to stop hugging,
a time to start looking and a time to stop looking,
a time to keep and a time to throw away,
a time to tear apart and a time to sew together,
a time to keep quiet and a time to speak out,
a time to love and a time to hate,
a time for war and a time for peace.*

———

Ecclesiastes 3:1-8 (NKJV)

> *To everything* there is *a season, A time for every purpose*
>   *under heaven:*
> *A time to be born, And a time to die;*
> *A time to plant, And a time to pluck* what is *planted;*
> *A time to kill, And a time to heal;*
> *A time to break down, And a time to build up;*
> *A time to weep, And a time to laugh;*
> *A time to mourn, And a time to dance;*
> *A time to cast away stones, And a time to gather stones;*
> *A time to embrace, And a time to refrain from embracing;*
> *A time to gain, And a time to lose;*
> *A time to keep, And a time to throw away;*
> *A time to tear, And a time to sew;*
> *A time to keep silence, And a time to speak;*
> *A time to love, And a time to hate;*
> *A time of war, And a time of peace.*

6 /

god puts eternity in our hearts and makes all things beautiful

---

He has made everything beautiful in its time. Also He has put eternity in their hearts... (Ecclesiastes 3:11 NKJV)

[context– Ecclesiastes 3:1-15 GW]

---

in the midst of life

When a severe earthquake hit the southern region of Sumatra in March 2005, my wife Susan and I were in the Philippines. Our son lived in Bengkulu, Sumatra when this 6.3 earthquake hit nearby. We heard the anxiety in his voice when he called us on his mobile phone. He told us he and his friends were evacuating to higher ground. He didn't want us to worry about him, but he probably wouldn't have mobile service for a while.

This was less than six months after the most destructive earthquake and tsunami in modern history destroyed Aceh, Indonesia, and devastated many coastal areas of the Indian Ocean. My wife and I saw the aftermath of that tsunami firsthand when we visited southern Thailand a month after it hit. We understood the power of a tsunami that follows a large earthquake. His call via mobile phone put the situation in context. On one hand, we understood the potential for danger. None of us had control of the situation. Yet we knew he was safe.

We may want to be good stewards of our environment and climate, but we can't control earthquakes, hurricanes, tornados, and volcanos. When we look at a slice of time when a catastrophe occurs, it's easy to become alarmed. We're concerned about what we can do at that moment. But when we look at a larger segment of time, we see how things have a way of resolving as people adjust and adapt to changes beyond their control.

The world has changed in dramatic ways over the past several decades. And yet, many things are as they've always been, especially human nature. The emergence of IT (information technology) enables us to know about and even see events and people in other parts of the world in real-time. This is both a blessing and a curse. It is a blessing that we can communicate with others halfway around the globe via Skype, Zoom, and other video mediums. But when we witness events taking place as "breaking news," we lack the context of being there in person, which can lead to fear and even panic.

When someone expresses thankfulness for life itself after enduring a disaster or tragedy, I'm reminded of God's goodness. His goodness shines through some of the darkest times the world has seen. How is it possible for a person to be thankful for their life after losing their home and possessions in a wildfire? How can people be optimistic in the aftermath of a devastating tornado or a major hurricane? Solomon's insights shed some light on this in the verses following his reminder of the purpose and significance of the cycles and seasons of life.

In the midst of life's events is life itself.

insights

After his observations of the ebb and flow of life's seasons, Solomon begins with a familiar lament, yet with encouraging insights.

> *What do working people gain from their hard labor? I*
> *have seen mortals weighed down with a burden that*
> *God has placed on them. (Ecclesiastes 3:9-10 GW)*

Though Solomon begins his reflections about life *under the sun* with a dark and dire tone, it seems to change here. Following his familiar lament, he gives two insightful observations related to time.

> *It is beautiful how God has done everything at the right*
> *time. He has put a sense of eternity in people's*
> *minds... (Ecclesiastes 3:11 GW)*

Solomon sees beauty in how God orchestrates everything according to His purposes. He observes how the events in all the cycles and seasons of life fit together in the fabric of life. As the seasons flow from one to another within a year across the backdrop of creation, God's purposes work together in a beautiful and complete way. Too often the saying—"you can't see the forest for the trees"—is true about our lives. We need to view our lives and the world as a tapestry of great beauty designed by God's creative hand. Solomon adds another remarkable statement that rings true—

> *He has put eternity in their hearts, except that no one can*
> *find out the work that God does from beginning to*
> *end. (Ecclesiastes 3:11 NKJV)*

This brief and poetic thought describes the yearning in us for something more—something greater than ourselves. Renowned missionary Don Richardson tells of universal awareness of God through what he called *redemptive analogies* in cultures and peoples throughout the world in his book,[1] *Eternity in Their Hearts*.[2] A redemptive analogy is a practice or belief within a culture that illustrates some element of the gospel.

Richardson and his family lived among the Sawi people of Irian Jaya (now called West Papua, Indonesia). His goal was to learn the unwritten language of the Sawi people so his family could share the gospel with them. It was a tremendous challenge. Especially when he realized the Sawi people viewed Judas, the betrayer of Jesus, as a hero. They considered treachery a virtue. Not only were the Sawi people illiterate, but they also warred with other tribes for the right to have the Richardsons live in their village.

Because of this danger to his family, Richardson decided they needed to move away from the tribe. This resulted in the Sawis engaging in a sacrificial ritual. One family brought an infant son to a family of the other tribe as a "peace child." As long as the child lived, there would be peace between the villages. This redemptive analogy was a great break-through for the Richardsons! He connected the Lord Jesus to the "peace child." Jesus was God the Father's "Peace Child." The Bible even declares God's Son to be the Prince of Peace (Isaiah 9:6).

Solomon points out what he came to realize through his reflections. Although God places a sense of eternity in each of us, none of us can grasp all of God's workings within eternity. After these insights, Solomon returns to the simple realization expressed earlier—

> *I realize that there's nothing better for them to do than to*
> *be cheerful and enjoy what is good in their lives. It is*
> *a gift from God…. (Ecclesiastes 3:12-13 GW)*

Instead of worrying ourselves by trying to understand all that takes place in the world and our lives, we need to enjoy what is good in our lives, even hard work. It's a gift from God. We're also reminded of God's greatness and our smallness, and this awareness is both necessary and intentional.

existential reflections for everyday life

The African American folk spiritual, "He's Got the Whole World in His Hands,"[3] which became popular in the late '50s, was first published in 1927.[4] Marian Anderson performed it at the March on Washington in 1963 where MLK Jr gave his noble speech, "I have a dream!"[5] Its origin reaches back to African American slaves working in the fields. As with so many spirituals, it was a song of assurance and hope born out of the dark drudgery of slavery. It was a song of faith, seeing beyond the burden of a hard life with no escape. God has the whole world and all people in it in His hands.

Solomon was a king of great wealth and power who owned many slaves. But even he couldn't escape the reality of his limited lifetime within eternity. He came to the same conclusion as those who were enslaved and denied freedom and saw death as their only escape from bondage.

We can see beyond the limitations of life on this earth with our perspective based on eternity. This ought to bring a sense of freedom into our hearts and minds, for God holds the whole world in His hands, even you and me. We are not adrift in eternity. God embedded eternity *in* us. All people have this whether or not they acknowledge it. God created us—all humanity—in His image. Our destiny is not an aimless life, but a life with purpose. We long for something more and something greater because God created us for a greater purpose than work or wealth. C. S. Lewis spoke of this longing when he said—

If we find ourselves with a desire that nothing in this world can satisfy, the most probable explanation is that we were made for another world. (from *Mere Christianity*)[6]

When we know there's more to our existence than the day-to-day routine of life, we can be content and know our lives have purpose and significance. Life *under the sun* does not limit us when we realize God embedded eternity in us.

Are you able to see the beauty woven into this world by God and beyond the burdens and hardships of this life?

When you need a fresh, unlimited perspective, just ask the Lord to reveal to you, or remind you, of His purpose for your life.

when upside down will be turned right-side up

I saw something else under the sun: There is wickedness where justice should be found. There is wickedness where righteousness should be found. I thought to myself, "God will judge righteous people as well as wicked people, because there is a specific time for every activity and every work that is done." (Ecclesiastes 3:16-17 GW)

[context– Ecclesiastes 3:16-22 GW]

enduring difficult times

I remember a time of perplexing difficulty as a young pastor. Looking back on that time, I realize how the Lord taught me to trust in Him rather than myself or the opinions of others. But my situation made little sense to me at the time and I didn't know how to handle it. About two years after the church began, I seemed to be attacked by various sources. Pastors of two different churches at each end of our town criticized me for polar opposite reasons. I also remember getting a call or two asking if we were a cult! I was neither equipped nor prepared for this type of attack. How should I respond? Or should I respond at all? As I was reading through the Bible about persecution, the Lord focused my attention on how Jesus handled such personal attacks. Here's what I read in 1 Peter 2:23—

> *When they hurled their insults at him, he did not retaliate; when he suffered, he made no threats. Instead, he entrusted himself to him who judges justly. (1 Peter 2:23 NIV)*

Criticism and personal attacks are hard to endure. But I can almost guarantee they will come your way, as they do for everyone else. Evil times and turmoil are also difficult to live through. When we see such things or are in the middle of them, many emotions get stirred up. We may go from anger to fear or from sadness to nostalgia. At some point, we may stop asking why. We just want it to end. But it doesn't just stop. A quick look at history reveals decades-long reigns of terror and times of turmoil. But we can also see when troublesome times resolve into times of peace. This is why we need to have a sense of perspective. We need to choose the long view over the immediate one. But how does a person do this?

How can any of us endure difficult times?

Sometimes the long view of perspective requires us to look back at what God has done in our lives and how God has dealt with wrong and wickedness in the past. We need to learn from history. One of my favorite reminders to help me do this is what King David did when tragedy struck the camp of his army of ragtag men. The Amalekites raided David's camp while he and his men were in Ziklag, doing their own raiding. Since the Amalekites took their wives and children captive while they were gone, the embittered men talked of stoning their leader, David. What did David do?

> *... David strengthened himself in the Lord his God. (1 Samuel 30:6c NKJV)*

David remembered God's faithfulness throughout his life. This encouraged and strengthened him in his spirit. Just read through the Psalms for more insight into the Lord's faithfulness to David. Just as King David "strengthened himself in the Lord," I learned to entrust myself and my concerns to God. I didn't need to respond or answer my critics. I needed to trust the Lord to deal with them. Israel's history reveals a clear narrative of God's faithfulness and His merciful and gracious nature towards an unfaithful people. Even when prophets warned of impending judgment because of Israel's unfaithfulness, their warning included an invitation to return to the Lord and a promise of restoration when they did (Malachi 3:7).

insights

As Solomon returns to his lament of life *under the sun,* he sees justice and righteousness perverted by wickedness. People who choose what is wrong and evil, upend what is right and just. We may expect widespread corruption at a simple level among petty thieves, but not from people in places of authority and responsibility. When people corrupt justice and pervert moral goodness, they live at a basic animal-like level. Animal-like instincts and desires drive them rather than their consciences. Their consciences become numb to what is just and right, even seeing evil as good. But Solomon sees the longer view. God is the ultimate judge of all. He works His purposes within His timing to set things in their right order.

God is who will turn what is upside down right side up.

Death is a certainty for all life on this earth. Here's how Solomon says it—

> *All life goes to the same place. All life comes from the ground, and all of it goes back to the ground. (Ecclesiastes 3:20 GW)*

Although Solomon doesn't speak of a resurrection from the dead, he hints at it in verse 21.

> *Who knows whether a human spirit goes upward or*
>   *whether an animal spirit goes downward to the earth?*
>   *(Ecclesiastes 3:21 GW)*

Only by a relationship with the Lord Jesus—who is the resurrection Himself—can we hope for our own resurrection from the dead beyond this life (John 11:25). Solomon summarizes his thoughts on all he says in chapter 3 this way—

> *So I perceived that nothing is better than that a man*
>   *should rejoice in his own works, for that is his*
>   *heritage. For who can bring him to see what will*
>   *happen after him? (Ecclesiastes 3:22 NKJV)*

We can be content with the life and work God gives us to do as we live by faith, trusting in Him. God holds the future in His hands. Ours included.

existential reflections for everyday life

Perhaps you wonder, how can we be content when things are in turmoil and when corruption and evil seem to prevail? This isn't logical and flies in the face of reason! This is where the long view of perspective is valuable. We can be content and confident in the future when we have genuine faith because of who our faith is in. God is consistent and faithful. He doesn't change with the cycles and seasons of life *under the sun*. He is trustworthy. We can be confident of His watchful care over our lives when our trust is in Him.

Things beyond our control are simply that—beyond our control. But they're not beyond God's control. He is sovereign—the ultimate authority over all. When we choose to place our lives in His hands daily, we can be content and confident. We may not know what the future holds, but as many have said before—*we know the One who holds the future.* It is wisdom on our part to put our lives in God's hands. We do this by faith. We trust in His sovereignty—His authority over all things and all people.

When we are not worried about tomorrow, we can be thankful for our lives each day.[1] We can take joy in whatever work God gives us to do. Unlike Solomon's reflections on life and death, those who trust in God by faith can look beyond this life with a living hope (1 Peter 1:3). Followers of Jesus have the assurance of a resurrection from the dead because of His resurrection (1 Corinthians 15:16-20).

Are you angry, fearful, or worried about the presence of evil and turmoil?

Are you concerned about the future, even your own?

If you choose to hold the long view of faith, it will help you put today, tomorrow, and eternity in the right perspective.

study questions for ecclesiastes chapter 3

For a more thorough study, read through Ecclesiastes Chapter 3 again to consider and answer the following questions broken into 2 sections—

Questions for Chapter 3:1-8—

1. What are the first and most obvious reminders of the cycles of life on earth?
2. What are the seasons of life that have a more emotional impact on your life?
3. How are strife and resolve seen as seasons within life?
4. How do each of these seasons and cycles help us have a better perspective on life?
5. Are there seasons in your life that are hard to accept or understand?
6. What is the season of your life right now? Do you see its value and purpose?
7. Are there situations in your life that need resolving? How will you pursue this?
8. Are you willing to trust God and seek godly wisdom for what you don't understand?

———

For Chapter 3:9-17—

1. How do these verses reflect the continuing tone of this book of wisdom?
2. What is said that counters this circular and cynical tone? How can these opposing thoughts exist at the same time?
3. Why would God want people to fear Him? What do you think is meant by this?
4. What are we told God will do concerning what is good and evil and when will this happen?
5. Are you able to see God's beauty in your life, the lives of others, and the world around you?
6. Do you find contentment in simple ways to help you navigate life's routines and difficulties?
7. Do you have a longing for the truth and a sense of hope? If not, do you know where to turn to get these?
8. How can respect and awe for God help us handle the anxieties and doubts that rise in our hearts and minds?

contentment is a handful of peace and quiet

One handful of peace and quiet is better than two handfuls of hard work and of trying to catch the wind. (Ecclesiastes 4:6 GW)

[context– Ecclesiastes 4:1-6 GW]

---

consumption doesn't breed contentment

We live five blocks from the beach. They built our house in the '80s and it is a prime candidate for renovation to be sold for a higher price. We live in an Airbnb paradise where many rentals become party house central for college students each summer. Not a week goes by without a postcard or a text sent by a realtor who wants to list our home for sale. Sometimes it's a flyer hung on the door or just a big card left on the porch. Their typical pitch is, "We can get you top dollar when you list with us!"

We see many older houses in our area torn down to build larger beach-style duplexes and empty lots are becoming scarce. In one block nearby, at least five large duplexes have gone up in the past few months. But this is our home. We don't want to sell it. It's become

"Nana and Papa's beach house," and a home for our parents in their last years. It's a gathering place for our family events and day-to-day visits. My wife and I hope to finish our last years here.

Consumerism and tourism drive America's economy. Two decades ago, economic experts estimated Americans consume about 25% of the world's goods, yet were only about 5% of the world's population.[1] Now, we comprise less than 5% (4.34% as of 2022), and our level of consumption continues to grow exponentially.[2] We consume a lot! But numbers don't tell everything and we can manipulate percentages to tell whatever story or support whatever ideology we choose.

Perhaps the most telling indicator of America's consumerism—more like our compulsion to consume and possess—is advertising. Whatever form of media you pick, the message is obvious. We want more! We deserve more! Advertisers feed and profit off our obsession to have more—food, clothes, nicer cars, bigger and better houses, and more wealth—just more!

Does all we have as a nation make us happy? No.

insights

To say Solomon was wealthy is a gross understatement. His wealth, power, slaves, and possessions were over the top. And yet, towards the end of his life, Solomon developed a nihilistic view of life. He said it's all, *"... pointless. It's like trying to catch the wind."* Even with all his wealth and power, he couldn't change the world and he couldn't change himself. Solomon felt it was better to never be born than to see the evil and oppression found in the world or to be stuck in the monotonous drudgery of work and life *under the sun.*

He even saw hard work and creative skills as just a source of rivalry with others, instead of the benefit of free will. Not only do we want more, but we also want to be better than others. It's almost as if he could foresee our present situation in western culture. A quick tour of Instagram seems to verify this is true for us, just as it was for Solomon.

But Solomon's nihilistic view of the world wasn't all negative. He came to appreciate the simple blessing of contentment with less for the benefit of peace. Solomon uses the image of "one handful of peace and quiet" compared to "two handfuls" of hard work and striving for more.

Just one handful of peace and quiet, can it really be that simple?

existential reflections for everyday life

Many people champion the expression "less is more" for different reasons. Essentially, it's a lifestyle choice. I'm not talking about minimalism, although that may have some virtue. I see this as more of a philosophy of life. The phrase "one handful" can mean something very different to different people. What a "handful" represents isn't about quantity or quality. Regardless of culture or status, we can choose to be content with "one handful" rather than pursue "two handfuls."

I grew up in a wealthy area even though our family wasn't rich. I saw beautiful homes filled with many unhappy lives. These were people who had more than "two handfuls." I've also lived overseas and visited many other nations in the world. I've seen people with very little material blessings able to enjoy their lives with a greater measure of happiness than many, if not most, wealthy people. Our family enjoyed a much simpler life overseas, even though our ministry work was typically 24-7, with few breaks. It's not to say there was no sadness or turmoil around us. There was. But the cultural lifestyle was simpler. It was more of a "one handful" way of life.

Since our return to our home culture in the US, we've tried to maintain a similar simplicity of life, but it's a challenge. However, it is worth choosing. Anyone can make the choice each day to be content with "one handful" or run with those who pursue the "two handfuls" way of life. Jesus had a very different outlook than Solomon, and Jesus knew and understood human nature (John 2:25). Jesus also believed in a "one handful" way of life and called His followers to pursue it.

> *(Jesus said) "If anyone desires to come after Me, let him*
> *deny himself, and take up his cross, and follow Me.*
> *For whoever desires to save his life will lose it, but*
> *whoever loses his life for My sake will find it.*
> *For what profit is it to a man if he gains the whole world,*
> *and loses his own soul? Or what will a man give in*
> *exchange for his soul?" (Matthew 16:24-26 NKJV)*

Ultimately, it's a choice each of us makes every day, whether by default or by decision.

> *Will you choose the "one handful" way of life or continue to pursue "two handfuls"?*

> *Are you willing to exchange "trying to catch the wind" for "peace and quiet"?*

When we choose the "one handful" way of life—a life of contentment, peace, and quiet—it may not change the world, but it will change us.

9 /
the cost of
loneliness and great
value of
relationships

Two people are better than one because together they have a good reward for their hard work. If one falls, the other can help his friend get up. But how tragic it is for the one who is all alone when he falls. There is no one to help him get up. (Ecclesiastes 4:9-10 GW)

[context– Ecclesiastes 4:7-12 GW]

the value of relationships

When our family moved overseas, we needed to adjust from our western culture to an Asian one. We learned how important relationships were in day-to-day life and the importance of the group or community over individual freedoms, identities, and rights.

After fifteen years overseas, we moved back to the US to a new place where our two sons lived. Initially, we struggled to adjust to our home culture because we missed the strong and dear relationships we developed within the community of our church fellowship and ministry work. Once again, we realized the importance and value of personal relationships. But loneliness knows no cultural or national boundaries.

Every person needs others. We are often at our best when in partnership with others. Even in a culture that values community over individualism, a person can feel lonely. God designed us for relationships. We—all humanity—are at our best when we have healthy connections with other people. When we speak of humanity, it is in a collective sense rather than an individualistic identity.

In America, we champion individualism and honor people whose individual accomplishments are greater than others. We call them VIPs—very important persons. We also have MVPs—most valuable persons or players. But the founding fathers of America saw the need for a more collective identity as a new nation. They saw the need for the thirteen separate colonies (states) to come together to form "a more perfect union."[1] America, as with any other nation, is stronger when united. The phrase—*united we stand, divided we fall*—echoes this. This was true at the founding of America, during its great Civil War, and it was a rallying cry for the nation during WWII.[2] This is not an exclusive American declaration. Many people in many places speak of this. It's a simple reminder of the value of community over individualism. While people of this western culture value individual identity and individual rights, the rest of the world values the collective identity of a group over individualism.

insights

Solomon tells us one more thing he sees as "pointless" *under the sun*— "people who are all alone." People who don't have children or family— those who care for them and whom they care for. And Solomon sees this as more by choice than circumstance—

> ... *there is no end to all the hard work they have to do.*
> *Their eyes are never satisfied with riches. But [they*
> *never ask themselves] why they are working so hard*
> *and depriving themselves of good things. (Ecclesiastes*
> *4:8 GW)*

As a pastor, I encountered many people in various life situations. I encouraged and prayed for many couples who couldn't have children of their own, and for singles who wanted spouses. This is hard to reconcile when some parents are selfish and irresponsible with their children, and when selfishness destroys a marriage bond. Often, it's less about circumstance and more the result of choosing self over others. Careers or wealth will never be enough without meaningful relationships. This is true for any selfish pursuit.

So, what's the remedy for loneliness? The remedy is to build and develop healthy relationships, friendships, and partnerships, and to find a place in community with others. Now more than ever, this is true.[3] Many people view verses 9-12 with marriage and family in mind, especially the line, *"… a threefold cord is not quickly broken."* But the context infers an even broader application (Ecclesiastes 4:9-12). Here's a brief look at how "two people are better than one"—

- *"a good reward for their work"* — As the saying goes, "Many hands make light work." It's often more enjoyable to work alongside another person and for a common purpose.
- *"If one falls, the other can help his friend get up."* — God's plan for the first man and woman was for them to be partners in life. Friendships and partnerships benefit us in many ways, especially when we need encouragement or help. We pick each other up in both figurative and literal ways.
- *"two people… together… can keep warm, but how can one person keep warm?"* — This illustrates how we can comfort and understand each other in a time of need rather than isolating ourselves when we are in a place of hurt or rejection. We all need comfort, reassurance, and understanding.
- *"… two people can resist one opponent."* — The obvious idea here is of protection and strength in numbers. Again, *united we stand, divided we fall.*
- *"A triple-braided rope (threefold cord) is not easily broken."* — Pastors often use this at weddings to illustrate how God is an important part of the union of husband and wife. It can also

apply to a family or community. Aside from the spiritual aspect, it's also a picture of teamwork.

How can these insights apply to our own lives?

existential reflections for everyday life

When God first created man, he was alone. God saw this wasn't good and created the woman as a companion and partner in life. This is the basis for the nuclear family, but also for a larger community. (Genesis 2:19-20). God never intended for any person to be alone, whether in relation to a family or inclusion within a community.

Relationships are the foundation of all humanity.

This is the model for the church—the Body of Christ and the Bride of Christ. It isn't one or the other, but both. Collectively, the church is the Bride of Christ (2 Corinthians 11:2; Revelation 21:2, 9). One believer isn't a church unto themself. As Jesus said,

> *"Where two or three have come together in my name, I am there among them." (Matthew 18:20 GW)*

Loneliness is often the result of continued choices to separate ourselves from others. It may be our reaction to abuse, insults, hurts, or rejection. These reactions may be reasonable for a while, but they can also be overreactions on our part. Choosing to withdraw from others as a means of self-protection may be wise for a time, but it can become a habit. Isolation can also be our preference for resolving conflicts and other difficulties. But as Solomon points out, isolation won't benefit us in the long run.

How do we resolve the problem of isolation and loneliness? We need to pursue relationships with others—preferably healthy ones! This may include marriage and family, but it isn't limited to those relationships. All of us benefit from healthy relationships. Life experience and psychologists affirm the value of personal relationships and confirm the harmful impact of loneliness.[4] Loneliness has a negative effect on our health and well-being—emotionally, physically, psychologically, and spiritually.

The remedy for isolation and loneliness is to be connected with others. But building and developing relationships requires a willingness on our part to not be the center of our own universe. As the apostle Paul said—

> *Don't act out of selfish ambition or be conceited. Instead, humbly think of others as being better than your-selves. Don't be concerned only about your own inter-ests, but also be concerned about the interests of others. (Philippians 2:3-4 GW)*

Of course, Jesus is the prime example and authority for us as believers. If we are to be His followers and have a continuing relationship with Him, we need to deny our selfish ways.

Do you struggle with loneliness?

Do you isolate yourself or seek comfort and encouragement from others?

Do you have healthy relationships with friends and family?

God's original design and intent for each of us is to be in relation-ship with Him and with other people. This requires us to look beyond ourselves and trust in God to help us build healthy rela-tionships.

is change the only constant in life?

But those who will come later will not be happy with the successor. Even this is pointless. It's like trying to catch the wind. (Ecclesiastes 4:16 GW)

[context– Ecclesiastes 4:13-16 GW]

"nothing is permanent except change"

I could hear the anxiety in my mom's voice before she told me about my dad. "I can't handle your dad anymore. He keeps falling down and I can't help him get up. I'll have to move him into a nursing home." I knew this call would come at some point, though I didn't know exactly when or what the situation would be. I also knew my dad wouldn't do well in a nursing home. The call came while we were in the middle of hosting a national pastor's conference, but we made the decision to move back to the US. We knew it was time. The Lord prepared us for this more than a year before. So, two weeks later, we arrived at our new house, in a new state, with what we could pack and bring with us on the plane.

Even though I knew what to expect, I wasn't ready for the major change in our lives when we moved back to our home culture after living in the Philippines for fifteen years. Previously, I worked with several cross-cultural missionaries to prepare them for re-entering their home culture after serving on the mission field, but I wasn't ready for what this change would bring. It's a major change. The change is not geographic so much as personal. Most people think overseas missionaries should be happy and excited about returning to their former homes. But that's just it. It's a *former* home. Life moves on, with or without us. The culture in our homeland also changes. But it isn't just that. *We* change. Cross-cultural missionaries typically learn this reality the hard way. We aren't the same people who moved away fifteen years earlier.

This isn't just true for cross-cultural missionaries—it's just more obvious for us. But life moves on even when we stay put in our home culture doing what we've been doing for years. The change in cultural values and life focus happens gradually. We don't notice the change because of our preoccupation with our own life priorities. But change happens. The ancient and obscure Greek philosopher Heraclitus appears to be the originator of the saying—*Nothing is permanent except change.*[1] Known for his metaphysical and obsessive focus on the constancy of change, he summed it up this way—"everything flows." Heraclitus would probably favor the book of Ecclesiastes since he echoes similar sentiments to Solomon's. His outlook on life and people was both paradoxical and dark.

Another expression of Heraclitus—*change is the only constant*—is a popular thought today. There's truth to this observation, but it doesn't need to be dark or discouraging. Change is a part of everyday life. Count on it! Things will change even when we want them to stay the same. Change takes place all around us, even when we feel stuck in a monotonous routine of life. The nature of life requires change. Growth and development are impossible without change.

We can be eager or resistant to change but not indifferent to it. When cultural and political change takes place, there's often significant resistance to it by those who prefer the status quo. And economic changes can produce anxiety or excitement depending on the outcomes. Unlike Heraclitus, some people pursue and see change as a general way to improve things. They embrace the idea of making change for the sake of change. But sometimes, the change we think we want isn't what we expect when it comes. This is what Solomon seems to allude to in these last four verses of chapter 4.

insights

These last few verses begin with a proverb—

> *A young man who is poor and wise is better than an old, foolish king who won't take advice any longer. (Ecclesiastes 4:13 GW)*

This sounds like an indictment of Solomon himself—a realization of his own foolishness, resistance to his advisors, and disloyalty to the Lord. It's a reflection of his life from youth to old age. Solomon was a young man of twenty years when he began his reign as the king of Israel. He was chosen to succeed King David over his older brothers (1 Kings 1:30, 2:12). Early in his reign, God gave Solomon extraordinary wisdom. But in his later years, Solomon became foolish. He collected hundreds of wives and concubines who turned his heart toward idolatry and self-gratification and away from the Lord (1 Kings 3:9-12; 11:1-5).

I believe Solomon had some sense of what would take place after his death. He seems to allude to this earlier concerning his legacy (Ecclesiastes 2:17-21). Perhaps he knew his son Rehoboam would not be a good ruler (he wasn't). The kingdom divided and another man who was not of royal birth (Jeroboam) ruled over the larger portion. Though we can't be certain this was in Solomon's mind, all this happened after Solomon's death (1 Kings 12).

From the beginning of Ecclesiastes, Solomon laments what he sees as an endless cycle of life and death on earth *under the sun*. As said too often, history repeats itself, and later generations forget those who've gone before them, even great people. Solomon knows that whoever succeeds him might enjoy the goodwill of people for a while, but it won't last. Leaders come and go. They may enjoy favor for a time but fall out of favor after a season. This is true of leaders in business, ministry, and politics. As a fellow pastor said of a new and apparent pastoral success in our town—"a new broom sweeps clean." Whether a product or a person, the new and different gains attention and favor at first, but it gets replaced with some newer, shinier object later.

Change for change's sake is an empty and shallow hope.

existential reflections for everyday life

When change is imminent, what is your usual response? If you know a specific change will take place and affect your life, do you feel anxious about it or excited? I'd guess most of us have some anxiety when we anticipate a change because of the general uncertainty that comes with change. Some people are influenced by what others say about an upcoming change, while others may be indifferent. Even if we think we aren't so influenced by others, it might surprise us how the opinion of others affects us.

When a popular product is updated to a newer version, there's a build-up to the release in order to create anticipation and excitement among avid fans. Various experts give their inside analysis and best guesses of what's coming. Devoted users of the product line up with excitement for hours for the release of the latest and greatest version. I see this whenever Apple or a similar company offers their new and improved laptop, phone, or watch.

With presidential elections, many people get tied up in knots with anxiety and worry over what the results reveal. And yet, decade after decade, the nation moves on with life. After change comes, even drastic change, life goes on. People adapt to new circumstances and situations, even in the direst of conditions. Often, the necessities of everyday life overcome whatever worries people had. And that shiny new product's newness wears off and life continues pretty much as it was before.

Change isn't just constant—it's inevitable. Whether we are eager for it or resistant to it, the change will come. But how we handle the constancy of change impacts our physical, psychological, and spiritual health.[2] The simplest and healthiest way to deal with change in our lives is to trust God with a continuing commitment to living by faith. He knows what's in the future and how it will impact us. Changes will come—in our lives and in the world. But as we entrust our lives and our concerns to the Lord, He will carry us through these times of change. I'm reminded of what Jesus said about this—

> *"So don't ever worry about tomorrow. After all, tomorrow will worry about itself. Each day has enough trouble of its own." (Matthew 6:34 GW).*

When you know changes are coming in your life, how does this affect you?

Do you often hope for or look for something new and different?

We can be certain that changes will come.

We can be confident in the One who holds tomorrow in His hands.

study questions for ecclesiastes chapter 4

For a more thorough study, read through Ecclesiastes Chapter 4 again to consider and answer the following questions—

1. What seems to be the motivation for people striving to achieve and working so hard? How does Solomon liken this?
2. What is a better alternative than working and struggling to get more?
3. What question does the single person who works hard never seem to ask themselves?
4. In what ways are two people better than one? What do you think this is emphasizing?
5. What motivates you in your life and work? Are you content with your work and life?
6. What do you enjoy most in your life? Why?
7. What place do people play in your life?
8. Are relationships more of a priority to you than work? If not, why not?
9. Who is important in your life? How do these relationships benefit you in your daily life?

11 /
a better life with fewer words and much fewer promises

Don't be in a hurry to talk. Don't be eager to speak in the presence of God. Since God is in heaven and you are on earth, limit the number of your words.

It is better not to make a promise than to make one and not keep it. (Ecclesiastes 5:2, 5 GW)

[context– Ecclesiastes 5:1-7 GW]

promises, promises, and too many words

Some of us talk way too much. We're asked a simple question but give a long-winded, detailed answer. It's called TMI—too much information. I know I'm guilty of this. And how often has someone said to you, "Hey, I thought you were going to call?" Or, "I thought you were going to come by?" Have you ever promised to pray for someone, had them thank you for praying for them when you see them next, then realize you forgot to pray for them? It's happened to me way too many times! And I know I'm not unique in this. We all make rash promises that we can't or won't keep. Good intentions may prompt us to make many promises, but do so with a lack of sound judgment or follow through. We make promises to call someone, go see them, and even pray for them. But too often, the immediacy and urgency of daily life push these promises out of our minds.

All of this carries over to our relationship with God. We make promises we can't or don't keep. And when we pray, it's a one-way conversation. We don't take time to listen or be still in His presence. When we do this, we are treating God as if He were just another person, and He is not. We are to have awe and respect for God because of who He is. This moves us to worship Him. It motivates us to honor Him rather than paralyze us with terror. The fear of God is not an anxious dread, as if He's angry with us and looking for a reason to annihilate us. To fear God is to revere Him (Proverbs 1:7; 2:1-9; 9:10; 15:33).

Our lives will be much better when our words are fewer and we don't make promises we can't or won't keep, especially in our relationship with God. We ought to fear God because of who He is—He is sovereign, all-knowing, all-seeing, and present everywhere at all times.

insights

Solomon gives us spiritual and practical advice in these opening verses of chapter five. It's easy to forget Solomon's reverence for God when reading through Ecclesiastes because of his cynical view of life and hardness of heart after his many wives and concubines turned his heart from loyalty to God. But we see his reverence for God in his request for a discerning and wise heart and at the dedication of the temple in Jerusalem (1 Kings 3:7-9 and 1 Kings 8).

Solomon bases his advice on experience—experience born out of failure. Although Solomon exercised great wisdom in his earlier years, he descended into cynicism because of his prideful sin. It's as if Solomon is pleading with his readers to learn from his mistakes. Here, he reminds us of what is primary and that enables us to escape the many snares of sin along the path of life *under the sun.*

First off, we're told—*"Watch your step when you go to the house of God..."* (Ecclesiastes 5:1 GW). This is an encouragement to show reverence for God in His house. The house of God in Solomon's time meant the courtyards and porches around the temple in Jerusalem, as it was in the days of Jesus. Now, we have various meeting places—from cathedrals to converted retail stores to homes. But this isn't about location in a geographic sense. It's about being in the presence of God. Notice the emphasis is on listening rather than speaking our own words, making promises or vows, or some form of sacrifice. As Samuel told King Saul—

> *"Has the Lord as great delight in burnt offerings and*
> *sacrifices, As in obeying the voice of the Lord? Behold,*
> *to obey is better than sacrifice,..."* (1 Samuel
> 15:22 GW)

A foolish person attempts to appease or please God with their many words, promises, and sacrificial offerings. But the Lord is much more interested in our hearts and attitudes toward Him than what we offer Him. When a person is anxious or worried, they may try to bargain or negotiate with God. "Lord, if you will do such and such, then I will never ask again." The caution is this—it's better not to make a promise or vow to God than make one and break it (Proverbs 20:25). Vows are solemn promises.

God is not a person whom we can manipulate or fool. He is God—our Creator, Redeemer, and Sustainer. Despite all our weaknesses and through the difficulties of life, we ought to fear God—to be in awe of Him and respect Him.

existential reflections for everyday life

How can this be practical and relevant to our lives? I believe these verses are just as relevant for believers today. I came to faith as a follower of Jesus at the beginning of the '70s Jesus Movement in Southern California.[1] It was a time when a more contemporary but genuine expression of worship replaced traditional religion. I recall singing Scripture-based praise and worship songs *a cappella* and led by our pastor, who would then teach us directly from the Bible. Many of us sat on the floor because the sanctuary was so crowded. Even then, it seemed sacred, and we could sense God's presence. In those early days, some church leaders would criticize the informality of our services. But now, those who prefer more informal worship criticize more traditional or sacred forms of worship. Neither view is right or wrong on its own. It should never be about a certain form of worship.

God has always sought people's hearts, not compliance with a certain form of worship. Jesus made this clear many times with the Jewish leaders who challenged Him (Matthew 9:13). Jesus also made this clear to a Samaritan woman who questioned Him about worship—

> *"God is Spirit, and those who worship Him must worship in spirit and truth." (John 4:24 NKJV) [see John 4:21-24 for context].*

My concern for the American church today is we too often emphasize doctrine above practice. We may know our doctrine and theology but fall short of living it out, so we fail to draw others to Jesus because they cannot see Him in us. Worship is more than music and public expressions of devotion. Worship is an attitude of the heart carried over to our daily lives and our interactions with others.

I served as a worship leader before serving as a pastor. Even when pastoring, I wore both hats many times and needed to segue from worship to preaching. So, I would ask the church body to wait quietly after our time of worship. I found this made some people uncomfortable. Silence, quiet, and waiting seemed alien to them. Sometimes, well-intentioned musicians would play their guitar or keyboard gently to fill in the silence, and I'd ask them to stop. We need to learn how to be still and quiet before God (Psalms 46:10).

I see this as an important takeaway from these first few verses in Ecclesiastes chapter five, and it prompts me to ask a few questions.

- *Do you fear the Lord with awe, respect, and worship?*

- *Do you take time to listen when you pray and worship, even if no one else does?*
- *Do you make promises to yourself, others, and God yet fail to keep them?*
- *When you pray, do you spend more time complaining, whining, or begging God for something rather than being thankful or interceding for others?*
- *Do you try to bargain with God instead of just trusting Him?*

These are all questions I need to ask myself from time to time. I hope you will too.

12 /
when wealth is more of a problem than a blessing

Whoever loves money will never be satisfied with money. Whoever loves wealth will never be satisfied with more income. Even this is pointless.

The sleep of working people is sweet, whether they eat a little or a lot. But the full stomachs that rich people have will not allow them to sleep. (Ecclesiastes 5:10, 12 GW)

[context– Ecclesiastes 5:8-17 GW]

poverty and redistribution of wealth

I'm thankful I grew up in a beautiful area where many wealthy people lived. Our family was middle class. We were neither poor nor rich. I remember trying to appear as if we were wealthy, but I had to work for whatever I wanted, unlike most of my friends. This gave me an opportunity to see the emptiness and futility of chasing after or having wealth. Even though our home life had its problems, we were a close-knit family. Many of my wealthy friends were envious of the stability of my family and home life. Though I thought I wanted what they had, they wanted what we had in our home. What irony!

Redistribution of wealth is a popular scheme to help solve the problem of poverty. But it won't. We cannot solve poverty with money. Poverty is an issue too deep for money to solve. Resentment toward the wealthy and an idealized philosophy is the root of wealth redistribution. The resentment is for good reason. Throughout history, the wealthy have wielded power and oppressed people to maintain their power and wealth. This is just as true in America's history, especially during the peak of the Industrial Revolution with wealthy magnates such as J. D. Rockefeller, J. P. Morgan, A. Carnegie, and C. Vanderbilt.[1]

Why do so many people resent the rich and the wealthy? They envy them. But Solomon tells us this envy of the rich is foolish. Riches and wealth never satisfy and bring problems the poor will never know. If anyone should know this, Solomon did.

There is a biblical basis for the redistribution of wealth, but it's a far cry from socialism or Marxism. It's not based on envy, nor on ideology. It's based on love and contentment. The first church redistributed their own wealth, but love and concern for one another was their motivation. As needs arose among them, they would sell what they had for the common good (Acts 2:44-45; 4:32-35). But it didn't last. Selfishness filled the hearts of a few and favoritism seemed to creep in. Poverty is more of a mindset than pure circumstance, and selfishness is at the heart of oppression and injustice.

insights

Solomon tells us the existence of oppression and injustice should not surprise us. He understood the nature of humanity to be selfish at its best and evil at its worst. He understood wealth and power, for he knew what it was to have it and yet be unsatisfied. This is the underlying reason for saying *life under the sun* was pointless. All these verses in the middle of chapter five focus on the problems of having wealth or lacking it. But Solomon reveals certain things about wealth that are misunderstood by those who don't have it.

Solomon's observation of oppression and injustice is just that—an observation. It's an age-old reality. Those in power over the poor use their power to their own advantage. But as unjust as this may be, Solomon acknowledges how dependent those in power are upon the labor of the poor. Even the king's food is a product of those who labor in the field. This is not a justification of oppression and injustice, but an observation.

"Sweet" sleep is the blessing of the laboring poor because of their honest labor. And yet, even though the powerful and wealthy seem to have all one could want, this "sweet" sleep eludes them. Solomon gives some insight into this baffling reality. Those who have riches can't take it with them when they die, just as righteous Job realized (Job 1:21). And the rich never seem to have enough. Worry consumes the wealthy, who hoard their riches. They worry about all they have and about losing it. As Solomon observed before, they also have to pass their wealth onto others whether they choose to do so or because misfortune takes it from them.

existential reflections for everyday life

When Jesus said there would always be those in poverty, it wasn't callousness. He knew the heart of humanity is selfish at its core (Mark 14:7-10; John 12:4-6). The problem with wealth or the redistribution of wealth is this—there will never be enough money to satisfy the heart of any person. At one point, John D Rockefeller owned 90 percent of the oil and gas industry in America.[2] When asked how much money would be enough, he said, "just a little bit more." Although many in the world think a little more money would satisfy them, the reality is this—it won't. This is what Solomon is trying to tell us in these verses.

What about a "little bit" of wealth redistribution? Having come of age in the '60s, then becoming a follower of Jesus in the early '70s, I've had some experience with communal living. I spent enough time in a few communal communities during the age of love-ins to see the reality beyond the rhetoric. Communal communities only work with good, fair-minded leadership, equitable organization, and cooperation. But this is rare. When it exists, it only lasts for a season.

What about the early church? The communal life of the first-century church only lasted for a short time. The early chapters of the book of Acts reveal this. Ultimately, some internal problems and external influences in the form of persecution disrupted the early church community. But here's the good news about this—even selfishness and persecution couldn't disrupt the genuine love true followers of Christ had in their hearts towards each other, the poor, and those who oppressed them. This was the earmark of true Christian believers as the church grew under persecution, political oppression, and pandemics. Though many were poor, they were known for their love, mercy, and grace.

Susan and I also had experience with a Christian communal community during the mid-seventies. It wasn't heaven on earth. It was hard work and had its share of problems. But God worked in us through it all. What we endured and learned in that season of life was of immeasurable value. In essence, it was the Kingdom of God on earth. This experience prepared us for the ministry God called us to in the following years as church planters and missionaries.[3] We've drawn upon what God poured into us during that season of life over and over the past thirty years. Thankfully, what God poured into us overflowed into the lives of others and bore fruit that honored God. Though we worked hard, our sleep was sweet. Even though we had little wealth in the eyes of others, we lacked nothing and experienced blessing after blessing.

What about you? Are you looking for "just a little bit more"?

Or have you learned to be content with what you have?

Oppression and injustice will continue because of selfishness, greed, and pride. But God blesses and honors those who trust in Him.

13 /
life's reward, god's gift, and a heart full of joy

At last I have seen what is good and beautiful: It is to eat and drink and to enjoy the good in all our hard work *under the sun* during the brief lives God gives us... It is a gift from God when God gives some people wealth and possessions... These people won't give much thought to their brief lives because God keeps them occupied with the joy in their hearts. (Ecclesiastes 5:18-20 GW)

[context– Ecclesiastes 5:1-20 GW]

a better understanding

Language is not always precise. Even when language is precise, people may not understand it. I learned this as a teacher overseas. Even when I took great care to explain things, students didn't understand what I said. Sometimes, people heard the opposite of what I intended. While teaching a workshop in the Philippines, my interpreter twisted my words to mean the opposite of what I said. It was not intentional on his part. My words were, "We need to understand what is in black and white in the Bible text." But my interpreter said,

"… either black or white." This is a common problem when using an interpreter.

What we say in one language within a culture rarely translates well into other languages and cultures. Some words and ideas don't translate at all. Our personal biases, our moods, and sentiments, along with our basic view of life, can also hinder our understanding of words. As so often noted, the optimist sees a cup as half full, and a pessimist sees it as half empty.

Words are like containers for concepts, feelings, or ideas. The context of spoken and written words provides keys to understanding these words. Even in their immediate context, people will misunderstand or misconstrue words. This is why people who only see literal meanings to words don't understand humor or satire. This was often the case when Jesus was with His followers and others who heard Him. Words can have more than one meaning, especially in varying contexts. Jesus spoke of "living water" to the Samaritan woman at the well and of Himself being "the Bread of Life" to those who were among the five thousand whom He fed (John 4:4-10; 6:35).

Countless people who've traveled from a developed nation to a developing or underdeveloped nation will say when they return home, "I didn't realize how good I have it in life!" Seeing the plight of others in desperate or difficult circumstances ought to help us realize "how good" we have it. But how much better would it be for all of us to realize what is good in our lives without comparing it to the lives of others?

Life is not a competition—it's a gift.

insights

Reading through Ecclesiastes, it's easy to get pulled along and discouraged by Solomon's view that "life under the sun is pointless". Yet here, Solomon shares simple insights and ways to avoid a cynical or depressing view of life. In the three verses at the end of chapter 5, Solomon shares three encouraging observations.

How we view life, especially our own life, can determine how we live our lives and cope with the challenges and routines of everyday life. A common role for counselors and pastors is to help people reframe their thoughts and actions toward a healthier outlook and better outcomes. This is what I see Solomon doing in these three verses. He reframes what may seem "pointless" and shows us a different way to see our life and the meaningful purpose for it.

Regarding the hard work a person endures within their brief life—it "is good and beautiful." This may seem contradictory to Solomon's previous observations, but he draws this conclusion after processing all he's seen *under the sun*. How can hard work in a brief life be "good and beautiful"? This is the glass-half-full view of life. Solomon says we are to enjoy whatever moments we can with whoever is in our life. This is like previous observations he made after speaking of life as pointless (Ecclesiastes 2:24; 3:12-13, 22).

Solomon also says it's *"... our lot in life."* But other Bible versions have a different take. The NKJV says it's our *"heritage"* and in the NET (New English Translation) it says, *"God has given them... their reward."* (Ecclesiastes 5:18 NKJV; Ecclesiastes 5:18 NET). Solomon speaks of the silver lining in the clouds like enjoying a beautiful sunset. He's not saying this is what you're stuck with. Those who have riches and wealth can enjoy them and accept and appreciate their role in life as a gift from God.

This realization is counter to what Solomon said in the verses preceding this observation. But he sees that when a person can be content and thankful, riches and wealth aren't a problem but a blessing from God. Solomon's third observation sums up the first and second ones. People who find contentment in their lives regardless of their circumstances don't worry and fret. Their hearts are full of joy instead.

existential reflections for everyday life

Being content and thankful while enjoying simple pleasures in life is a way to reframe our lives toward a positive outlook. Contentment and thankfulness are not emotions like happiness. They are grounded deeper in the attitude of our hearts and in a healthy mindset. Happiness is not the same as joy. Happiness is an emotion dependent on circumstances or situations. Joy comes from a deeper place in us. It is more spiritual than emotional (John 16:22; Galatians 5:22).

One of my favorite movies is *Life is Beautiful.*[1] It illustrates the power of reframing. The story begins in the Tuscany region of Italy preceding WWII. It's both a comedy and drama following the life of a Jewish bookstore owner and his family. After being forced into a concentration camp, the father uses his imagination to reframe the family's dire circumstances as a game of intrigue. He reframes the evil of the camp and the war so that *Life is Beautiful.*

> **But how can we reframe our lives to see what is "good and beautiful"?**

We can do this with the little things in life. Special moments and simple blessings and pleasures can help us reframe our lives in a positive way. We can *choose* to be content and thankful. Here are a few ways I do this in my life—

- Daily prayer that begins with giving thanks
- Devotions with my wife in the early morning
- Keeping in touch with and enjoying time with our children and grandkids
- A walk at sunset (or sunrise)
- Walking or riding a bike on the beach
- Simple conversations over coffee or a meal with friends

That's my shortlist to help me reframe my life to see the beauty and blessings God gives me. Hopefully, this gives you an idea of how to reframe your life to see what is *"good and beautiful."*

Why not take some time to make your own life-reframing list?

What and who are you thankful for?

What are the simple pleasures you enjoy?

How can you begin and end each day to reframe your life in a positive way?

If you focus and dwell on what is dark, discouraging, or disturbing in your life and the world around you, your life will be like a cup-half-empty.

When you reframe each day in your life with what's good and beautiful and acknowledge God's gifts in your life—then your heart can be filled with joy!

study questions for ecclesiastes chapter 5

For a more thorough study, read through Ecclesiastes Chapter 5 again to consider and answer the following questions broken into 2 sections—

Questions for Chapter 5:1-7—

1. What are the first admonitions Solomon gives here?
2. What is recommended and why?
3. When should we limit our words? What tends to happen when we speak too many words?
4. What are we told about promises and God?
5. What advice is given and why?
6. When we fail to keep our word and follow through on things, what is the wise thing to do?
7. Do you find yourself making promises to assure people of your intentions?
8. Do you ever regret making promises, or have a hard time keeping the ones you make?
9. How do you guard yourself against making rash promises or talking too much?
10. When was the last time you listened more than talked, especially in God's presence?

For Chapter 5:8-20—

1. What are two or three specific things said about those who have and love wealth?
2. Who seems to enjoy rest and sleep more—those with much or those with little? Why?
3. What is the status of all people at birth and death? How does Solomon liken the pursuit of wealth?
4. What seems to be the key to enjoying life regardless of a person's status in this life?
5. What causes you to lose sleep most often?
6. Do you realize what causes you anxiety or worry?
7. When was the last time you had a good night's sleep?
8. Which do you experience more of—inner peace or stress?
9. Have you ever gotten something you longed for, only to be disappointed with it?
10. How do you escape or deal with the cares and desires of life?
11. Do you handle the cares and desires of your life in a healthy or unhealthy way?
12. What do you see would help you live a more content life?

14 /
the deep dark pit of selfishness and self-pity

There is a tragedy that I have seen *under the sun*. It is a terrible one for mortals...

No matter how long he would have lived, it still would have been better for him to have been born dead...

Even if the rich person lives two thousand years without experiencing anything good—don't we all go to the same place? (Ecclesiastes 6:1, 3, 6 GW)

[context– Ecclesiastes 6:1-6 GW]

how selfishness and self-pity become dark

My wife and I raised four children. We raised our children immersed in church life and knowledge of the Lord. As they came of age, they made their own confessions of faith. We love our children. They learned how to show affection and acceptance to one another through our example and guidance. They also gained a sense of responsibility as members of our family and for one another through regular household chores. Our involvement in full-time ministry provided plenty of structure in their lives. Perhaps more than they would have chosen for themselves.

As much as we loved them from birth to adulthood and beyond, they had one common characteristic. They were all selfish, just like their parents, and our parents, and all the people on the face of the earth— past, present, and future (Romans 5:12-14). Our children grew up to pursue their own lives and continue in their faith to this day. Now we have seven grandchildren. And you know what? We love them a lot! But they are also selfish, like their parents and their grandparents (us).

The most common trait of humans is selfishness. We see selfishness in its purest form in children. Selfishness isn't evil. It's a focus on ourselves—a sense of our singular identity. Selfishness is a common trait that connects and separates us at the same time. It connects us since it's common for us all. But it separates us because we are all different. Each of us has our own identity. We have different likes and dislikes. We prefer one thing over another. Young children illustrate this well. One child wants to eat mac and cheese, while the other wants a burger. One child prefers apples while another loves strawberries. At this simple level of preference and dislikes, selfishness isn't much of a problem—it's only a bother for the parents.

Selfishness becomes a problem when the preferences or choices of one person or group of people oppose and infringe upon the rights and privileges of others. Then selfishness can become abusive and oppressive. With children, one child bullies or manipulates another. But with adults, bullying magnifies. We see a perfect illustration of this magnification in politics and the recent cancel culture, especially when it turns abusive and violent.

Selfishness also becomes a deep pit when it evolves into self-pity. Self-pity can appear passive at first, but it can easily turn aggressive and violent when unchecked. When a young child throws a tantrum because they want their own way, it may seem comical or amusing. But when a tantrum spills over into rage, a person may become violent towards themselves or others. Depression and self-pity, which bring a sense of hopelessness, may also result in suicide. This is an oversimplified view, but suicides and murders often result from self-focused hate and rage.

When selfishness and self-pity go unchecked, they become a deep, dark pit.

insights

Once again, Solomon returns to his cynical view of life in relation to a person's wealth. Does it seem contradictory to what he concludes at the end of the fifth chapter? It is. Solomon returns to his lament about the unfairness of life when it ends, as he complained before about a rich person's wealth going to others after death (Ecclesiastes 2:17-23; 5:13-17). But here, it takes a darker turn.

Solomon compares death's inevitable impact on the life of a wealthy person to a stillborn child. He adds a second question to the first one asked at the beginning of Ecclesiastes. Until now, Solomon's underlying question is, *What's the point of life on earth?* Now, he extends this by asking, *What's the difference between a stillborn child's existence and what appears to be the full life of a wealthy person?* It's important to notice how Solomon frames these two questions. First, Solomon sees a great tragedy in life *under the sun—*

> *"There is a tragedy that I have seen* under the sun. *It is a terrible one for mortals." (Ecclesiastes 6:1 GW)*

Another version uses the word *evil* instead of *tragedy* in this first verse. Solomon then questions the value of life itself. He sees the rich man who can't enjoy his wealth and who loses it all in death as no better off than a stillborn child. He says, the stillborn child only knows darkness but finds more rest than the rich man. A third way Solomon frames this terrible tragedy is with a what-if scenario. He gives us a hypothetical question, not an accurate observation.

> *Suppose a rich person wasn't satisfied with good things while he was alive and didn't even get an honorable*

burial after he died. Suppose he had a hundred chil-
dren and lived for many years. No matter how long he
would have lived, it still would have been better for
him to have been born dead. (Ecclesiastes 6:3 GW)

This is a very dark and cynical view of life. Solomon is seeing this from an earthly viewpoint. This earthly view of life excludes God and holds no hope of anything but life from birth to death. This is the view of the atheist, and it is also the view of modern existentialist philosophy. It is a hopeless view. It is a view of life without the hope of resurrection from the dead.

When we compare our lives to the lives of others, we can easily fall into a negative perception of what they have or don't have that's different from our life. Sadly, this is a problem among pastors. When meeting with other pastors at a gathering or conference, they'd often ask me how many people attended our church. Somehow, a higher attendance was a gauge of success. This is way too common. It's perpetuated by people in the church much the same way as hearing children brag their dad could beat up another's dad.

Why does this measuring stick of attendance comparison continue? Because we feed into this type of measuring ourselves against others to make us feel better about ourselves. What happens when we don't measure up? You guessed it. We feel less than others. This often spurs questions about our abilities and value as a person. Those questions then result in embarrassment or shame.

I know this to be true. This plagued me as a pastor in my earlier years of the pastorate. The only way to escape it is by not taking part in the comparison game. When we question the value of life based on the negative perception of our own life, we descend into a pit of darkness that gets deeper and deeper as we pity ourselves with envy or hate for others. This is how selfishness and self-pity become a deep, dark pit.

existential reflections for everyday life

We are all selfish by nature. We were born with it. And we all feel sorry for ourselves. The only way to keep selfishness and self-pity from growing into a deep, dark pit is by maintaining a healthy perspective. In order to do this, we need to be grounded in the truth about ourselves, life, the world, and God.

The truth is neutral. It's not based on feelings or immediate circumstances or the opinion of people. We need to accept the truth about who we are. We don't need to be the best-looking, strongest, wealthiest, most popular person, or whatever other measurements we use to compare ourselves to others. Based on these comparative metrics, there will always be someone who is more this-or-that than us.

We need to avoid getting sucked into the comparison game. Such comparative measurements are subjective and change with time and the swings of culture. You set yourself up for failure when you base your perception of the world around you on what cable news networks and social media put out. The projected darkness in this world will get more intense. Count on it!

How can we avoid falling into this deep, dark pit? Sometimes, the simplest way to get a fresh and rational perspective on life in this world is to take a walk, enjoy some sunshine or time in nature, reflect on the good things in your life, and be thankful.

If you want the truth about God, read His written Word—the Bible. Find a readable Bible version and just read. The Gospels are a good place to start and either Psalms or Proverbs are good, too. If reading isn't your thing or is difficult for you, you can listen to it for free. The YouVersion Bible app has many versions available in audio, such as the ESV, NIV, or NKJV.[1] As you read or listen, think about what you're reading or listening to and take some notes. You can meditate on or prayerfully process what God's Spirit brings to your attention.

How do we keep from falling into the deep, dark pit of self-ishness and self-pity?

Life has purpose and value because it's a gift from God.
Don't focus on yourself or your circumstances. Don't focus on
or compare yourself to others.

**Focus on the Lord and His goodness, and enjoy the beauty of all
He's created.**

15 /

the frustrations and questions of an unsatisfied life

Everything that people work so hard for goes into their mouths, but their appetite is never satisfied.

It is better to look at what is in front of you than to go looking for what you want. Even this is pointless. It's like trying to catch the wind.

Who knows what may be good for mortals while they are alive, during the brief, pointless days they live? (Ecclesiastes 6:7, 9, 12 GW)

[context– Ecclesiastes 6:7-12 GW]

satisfaction guaranteed?

I don't trust advertisements. I'm probably not alone in this. But we're kind of stuck with some form of advertising. Even if you can cut them out of what you watch on TV (or cable or whatever), it's hard to get away from billboards along the road. Even on our cell phones, most apps include ads unless you pay for the "premium version." Most magazines and newspapers (for those who remember them) are filled with ads to pay for their publication.

Many of the newer ads, especially on TV broadcasts, feature a story-telling motif. One car company always seems to have families with dogs. We see the dog aging with the people while the car seems to outlast everyone else. Some ads have silly story scenarios. They all attempt to build trust. Somehow, all this marketing is to assure us that buying whatever they're selling is a wonderful decision.

And then, there are those obnoxious ads that over-promise. I'm sure you've seen more than a few advertisements with promises like, "Satisfaction guaranteed or your money back!" I think the advertisers are confident most people won't bother returning the product to get a refund even though they're not satisfied. Hmm, that reminds me. I'm still waiting to experience "the best night of sleep" that I've ever had on that especially overpriced pillow. I think most of us don't expect to be "100% satisfied." We accept disappointments as part of everyday life. We realize satisfaction is relative and happiness is temporary.

The idea of satisfaction has a low threshold for most people on the face of the earth. If there's enough food for the day, shelter from the elements, and relative safety, this satisfies most people, or at least it relieves them of worry. The expectation of satisfaction in life is more of a first-world concern than what I call most of the rest of the world.[1] I've seen that many people who live at the poverty level are often more content and satisfied with their lives. Why? Because they have lower expectations, and their lives are simpler than we who live in more developed western nations.

Amazingly, this is the case for many people living in subsistence poverty, also known as *absolute poverty*.[2] It's also referred to as *relative poverty*, which is much lower than America's nationally calculated poverty level. I don't want to make light of the problem of poverty in the world or in my nation. Poverty is real and a real problem.

Still, having more doesn't always bring satisfaction to a person's life. Western cultures and nations, especially America, are typically more concerned with more self-absorbed needs as echoed in a 1965 rock and roll song—"I can't get no, satisfaction!" First-world problems are trivial compared to having basic personal needs met.[3] We ought to ask ourselves on what we base our level of satisfaction. Is it what we lack, want, or need?

What we complain about often indicates how self-absorbed we are. In the ancient world until the middle of the twentieth century, only the wealthy and privileged were concerned with what we now consider inconveniences. The wealthy had expectations of more than the necessities of life. But from the 1950s on, as we recovered from a global economic depression and the Second World War, more and more people experienced opportunities and affluence once reserved for the wealthy. Perhaps longing for "the good old days" isn't so much about nostalgia as a longing for a simpler way of life.

insights

In the second half of Ecclesiastes chapter six, I see five frustrations and questions expressed by Solomon—a man unsatisfied with *life under the sun*. First, our bodies need fuel to function properly, and that fuel is food. But how much food do we need and what foods are best for our bodies? Of course, opinions abound in answer to these questions, but one thing is certain—many people in developed countries eat more than their bodies need. And what we eat isn't always healthy for us. Working for food and other basic needs is wise and a reasonable motive for work (Proverbs 16:26). But the basics rarely satisfy us. We want more and this leads to dissatisfaction in our lives. As it says in another version—*"And yet the soul is not satisfied"* (Ecclesiastes 6:7 NKJV).

This sets the tone for the remaining verses. Solomon also returns to thoughts expressed earlier in Ecclesiastes. He questions if the rich have an advantage over the poor in navigating life's journey and interactions with people (Ecclesiastes 2:15). The poor have less to lose when disasters take place, but they are more likely to help their neighbors than those who are wealthy. Solomon sees the benefit of contentment with what a person already has rather than seeking more. Another Bible version puts it this way—*Better what the eye sees than the roving of the appetite* (Ecclesiastes 6:9 NIV). This reminds me of what's called

FOMO (fear of missing out),[4] and Solomon says—*This too is meaningless, a chasing after the wind.*

In verse 10 of chapter six, Solomon reaches back to the famous expression—*"there's nothing new under the sun"* (Ecclesiastes 1:9-11), and he adds a reminder—*"And he cannot contend with Him who is mightier than he"* (Ecclesiastes 6:10 NKJV). We can understand this in two ways. First, there will always be others who are greater than us in authority, power, and strength. But I believe Solomon refers to God, who is greater than all. The last two verses of chapter six echo Solomon's thoughts at the beginning of chapter five. Speaking less and listening more is of greater value and usefulness than the other way around. And for all the talk, questioning, and theorizing we may do, only God knows the future.

existential reflections for everyday life

Comparing our lives with others is a sure path to dissatisfaction and trouble, as I've shared before. It leads to more frustrations and an unsatisfied life. This makes us and those around us miserable. Frustrations are common to all of us. What's different for each of us are the sources of our frustrations. What bothers and frustrates me probably differs from what bothers and frustrates you or someone else. Disappointments lead to frustrations. But what causes our disappointments?

Most disappointments result from unmet expectations.

Some expectations are reasonable and realistic. When we work for an agreed wage, we expect to get paid the same when we finish the work. When we order an item from a menu at a restaurant, we expect to receive what we ordered. But things don't always go as expected. While overseas, my wife ordered a hamburger but received a cheeseburger. When she told the server about the mix-up, the server explained, "I'm sorry ma'am, we're out of ham." My wife's restaurant experience resulted from a misunderstanding of culture and language. Living overseas taught us the need to adjust our expectations to the reality of life as it is. Just because an expectation seems reasonable to us doesn't mean it is realistic.

The frustrations and questions that bothered Solomon, as expressed in these verses, were the consequence of his unmet expectations. God gave Solomon great wisdom. It was his own failures and limitations that frustrated him. But Solomon's expectations of knowing and understanding all there is to know and understand were unreasonable and unrealistic expectations. Solomon's frustrations and questions resulted from his limitations as a human. But such things are common to us all. And these disappointments and mysteries can lead us all to an unsatisfied life if we let them.

How can we overcome the frustrations and mysteries of life under the sun? How can we avoid what leads to an unsatisfied life? We can choose to approach life in a different way. Here are a few suggestions based on Solomon's previous conclusions and my own life experience.

- Choose to trust God with your life and whatever is beyond your understanding (Proverbs 3:5-6).
- Learn to be content with what God provides, whether it's a little or a lot (Philippians 4:12).
- Choose to humble yourself and do what is good and just (Micah 6:8).
- Choose to make people more of a priority than material things in your life.
- Live as simple a life as you can.
- Do more listening than talking, be thankful rather than complaining, and be an encourager rather than criticize.

Susan and I have learned the value of these suggestions from our time in ministry in the US and overseas. These are decisions and choices we need to make each day. These are *my* suggestions.

Now consider what would help *you* live a satisfying life.

study questions for ecclesiastes chapter 6

For a more thorough study, read through Ecclesiastes Chapter 6 again to consider and answer the following questions—

1. What does Solomon see and lament as a tragedy?
2. What does Solomon see as a common pursuit eluding people who live on the earth?
3. What seems to be like "trying to catch the wind"?
4. Why do you think this expression is used so often in Ecclesiastes?
5. In all Solomon says about "pointless" talk and days, who would be stronger than us, "mortals"?
6. What seems to lead to a sense of hopelessness in *your* life?
7. How do you cope with the routine of life? Do you like or struggle with it?
8. What are ways you find solace and hope within the routines in your life?
9. How do you see beyond hopelessness and cynicism, or are you able to?

16 /
a sober perspective based on inverted wisdom

The minds of wise people think about funerals, but the minds of fools think about banquets.

Don't ask, "Why were things better in the old days than they are now?" It isn't wisdom that leads you to ask this! (Ecclesiastes 7:4, 10 GW)

[context– Ecclesiastes 7:1-10 GW]

changing and unchanging wisdom

I remember my first philosophy class. I could tell right away it was all about being able to defend your position on various topics. And when your opinion didn't line up with the teacher's, you'd better be ready for a dressing down in front of the class.

I grew up in a family where dinner discussions took priority over dinner itself. I learned early on to defend my position on various topics. This helped me and hindered me in school. On one hand, debating an issue wasn't foreign to me as it might have been for other younger students. But this set me up for failure with those who used more polished reasoning, including those with a broader understanding of philosophy.

The word *philosophy* is an anglicized version of a Greek compound word with a literal meaning—*love of wisdom*. Wisdom is a broad subject. A narrow definition of wisdom is *insight* or *understanding*. But the subject of wisdom is broad because of how the word is applied and the focus of its application. Philosophic wisdom focuses on varying ethical and moral values. Theological wisdom studies biblical and spiritual beliefs. There's a broad spectrum within the fields of philosophy and theology because of the beliefs and values of the people who develop various philosophical and theological views.

It is said that scientific knowledge and wisdom are based on empirical evidence—observable and definitive proof. As scientific knowledge develops, so do the conclusions of scientists. But here's some historical perspective. "Authoritative experts" once believed the earth was flat and bloodletting with leeches was a common medical practice until the late eighteenth century. General awareness of world history reveals great swings in the beliefs and values of humanity. We can see this from the times of the Dark Ages to the Renaissance, and then came the Age of Enlightenment, along with the significant change from agrarian to industrial economies.

During these major shifts in the world, religious, philosophical, and political views also changed. Commonly held wisdom also changed with these shifts in history and culture. We refer to these varying views of wisdom as conventional or prevailing wisdom—the majority view of insight and understanding that influenced beliefs and values.[1] Human wisdom changes. It is not absolute. Conventional or prevailing wisdom changes with cultural changes. What doesn't change is human nature.

We are self-centered and selfish by nature, which makes human wisdom unreliable.

But true godly wisdom doesn't change because God is unchanging in

His nature. Solomon declares this simple truth at the beginning and throughout the book of Proverbs —

> The fear of the Lord is the beginning of wisdom, And
> the knowledge of the Holy One is understanding.
> *(Proverbs 9:10, NKJV)*

insights

At first glance, these verses at the beginning of chapter seven have a morbid tone. We might wonder, "Why so much focus on death?" The short answer—life is short. This is an important emphasis through the overall message of Ecclesiastes. Currently, the average life expectancy of a person in the US is about eighty years.

Do you remember your perception of chronological time when you were a child? I can remember wanting to get to certain ages so that I'd be able to go to school, drive a car, graduate, and so on. I also remember being bored with school in later years. Driving a car was fun at first, but the responsibilities mounted up when our family grew along with my errand list. Even before each graduation and accomplishment, we look ahead to what is next.

As we get older, time seems to go faster and the years seem to slip by before we're ready to let them go. This became noticeable to me when our children reached high school. I didn't want them to grow up so fast! Now with grandkids, they seem to grow at hyper-speed. But we can't slow the pace of life down, nor can we extend it. This underscores the reality that life is short.

There is a simple progression from verse 1 to verse 10 in this chapter. It begins with a focus on the shortness of our lives, moves to some proverbial thoughts related to our character, then to a sober sense of perspective on life itself. It's a snapshot of the speculative wisdom of Ecclesiastes. The first few verses start with a morbid perspective to remind us of the importance of moral character—"a good name." A common theme throughout the book of Proverbs is the contrast between wisdom and foolishness. We find a key thought at the end of verse 2—"Everyone who is alive should take this to heart!"

The next few verses focus on a contrast between the wise and foolish, with a reminder of the danger to our souls of corruption. But verse 3 leads us to a clearer understanding of these ten verses—*"sober reflection is good for the heart"* (Proverbs 7:3 NET). By "sober reflection," we see the thought of verse 2 extended, and this leads us to verse 10—

> *Don't ask, "Why were things better in the old days than they are now?" It isn't wisdom that leads you to ask this! (Proverbs 7:10 GW)*

Nostalgia is nice, but it is deceptive. When we focus on "the old days" as better, it's a matter of selective memory. Again, we should all take to heart the simple reality that life is short.

existential reflections for everyday life

Most of us have fleeting thoughts about our younger selves, especially as we get older. More than a few people have remarked on how we view things in life now through the lens of our much younger selves. When I watch my grandson play sports, I think of the times I played sports with his dad and uncle as a young parent. But now when I pick up a ball to throw or kick a soccer ball, my body reminds me how much time has passed from then to now. High school reunions are friendly reminders of the deceptiveness of nostalgia, especially with the 30th, 40th, and 50th-year reunions. I went to one of my high school reunions. We wore name tags with our senior photo and name, but these photos didn't match the faces and bodies that wore them. Nostalgia crashed into reality!

How can we make sense of this inverted wisdom for our own lives? First, look at what Solomon points out as important priorities. Beginning in verse 1, he reminds us of the importance of integrity in character, a sober reflection on life, the value of wisdom, listening to a wise rebuke instead of flattery, humility with patience instead of anger or pride, and rejecting nostalgia for a truer perspective on life.

Think of this as inverted goal setting. Our goal isn't death—it's the life we live each day between now and whenever our life will end. Of course, none of us knows when our death will come, no matter how much planning we do or what precautions we take to prevent premature death. When we have a deadline for finishing a project, we set priorities, schedule our time, and work towards completing the project the best we can. Every life has a deadline –literally. But that's not the point of Solomon's morbid view of life. It's the opposite. Solomon gives us inverted wisdom.

What would you do with your time if you knew you only had six months to live? What or who would you put your focus on? How would you prioritize your time and energy? The answers to these questions may reveal the substance of your life. If you committed yourself to having as much fun as you can, enjoying as many pleasures as possible, or something else along these lines—what would this reveal about you? I asked my wife this question. She told me her priorities would be —to spend as much quality time as possible with her family and the Lord. Her priorities would be simple, personal, and doable. There may be no right or wrong answers to these hypothetical questions. But with all the uncertainties in life, it might be a good thing to take an inventory of your life and make some changes. Here are some things you could ask yourself—

- *What are your priorities in life?*
- *What do you spend most of your time, energy, and resources on?*
- *Who is important to you?*
- *How much time do you invest in sharing quality time with the people who are important to you?*
- *Where do things stand with you and your Creator?*
- *Are you ready to meet Him face to face?*

If it were me, I'd start at the bottom of this list and work my way up. But that's what I would do.

What about you?

wisdom to grasp a conundrum beyond our control

Consider what God has done! Who can straighten what God has bent? When times are good, be happy. But when times are bad, consider this: God has made the one time as well as the other so that mortals cannot predict their future. (Ecclesiastes 7:13-14 GW)

[context– Ecclesiastes 7:11-18 GW]

---

atheism, religion, and spirituality

I was never an atheist, nor was I inclined toward religion, especially as I came of age. I was interested in spirituality. Most of this interest coincided with my use of psychoactive drugs and the culture of my youth. I've written about this in various posts and in my first book.[1] I was searching for the truth, and though I realized Jesus was most important, I had questions. Some of those questions went unanswered for about two years. Apparently, my questions were too philosophical for some believers to answer. This left me adrift until I began reading the Bible every day. Though I understood little of what I read, God made Himself known to me little by little.

I know atheism, as well as agnosticism, appeals to many people just as religion and spirituality do for others. Atheism's appeal may simply be its focus on humanity as the end-all-be-all explanation for life. The answers to life and everything else reside in humanity, so there's no need for God. Most atheists claim people result from a cosmic incident that somehow brought them into existence.

Religion's appeal is nearly the opposite of atheism. In religion, there's an answer for everything because of God's existence and power. Many religious people believe God guides us and even determines our human will. I see spirituality or spiritualism on a different plane from religion. Everything is spiritual in its origin. All existence—whether animate or inanimate—is ultimately spiritual in its existence. But in spiritualism, a person is still the master of their own will and existence.

Atheists see the physical world and human reason as the sum of all things. Spiritualists see themselves as unrestricted to the physical world. They see their existence and destiny extend beyond what is physical. What about those who trust in religion? Mostly, they see their lives restricted by God in the physical world and beyond life on earth.

It may seem that religionists hold a more balanced view of life and God, but this would be a hasty conclusion to draw. The inverted wisdom of Solomon's existential reflections in Ecclesiastes seems to poke holes in the beliefs of these three general perspectives. A person may find themself inclined towards one view of life over the others, but neither of them may be the wisest path for life. I'm thankful for how God drew me out of a hazy spiritual path into a personal relationship with Him.

insights

Solomon returns to a few themes from previous chapters and adds some proverbial wisdom in this segment of verses in chapter seven. Wisdom is to be valued over inherited wealth. Although wealth may indicate family stability and strength, wisdom is helpful even for those without a family inheritance. Wisdom provides a means of protection as a defense against injustice and foolishness. Its greatest value is giving life to those who have wisdom. How? The knowledge and understanding of wisdom will lead a person to a life that benefits them and honors God.

Solomon then reminds us that only God can "straighten what He bends." We are not stronger or wiser than God. We need to be wise enough to recognize God's sovereign power overall. As Solomon said in chapter three, there is a season and purpose for everything we experience in this *life under the sun*. Whether a situation in life seems good or bad to us, God has allowed both to take place. This is a reminder that no one can predict the future.

Solomon observes a conundrum none of us understands.

Why do some people who live virtuous lives seem to die too soon, while others who are evil live longer? None of us, including wise Solomon, understand this. It seems unfair and pointless. After observing this conundrum, Solomon dispenses some more inverted wisdom. First, he tells us not to make ourselves miserable by trying to be too virtuous and wise. Likewise, we are not to be wicked and foolish, which will lead to an unprofitable life and premature death. Perhaps the most puzzling of Solomon's statements is this—

> *It's good to hold on to the one and not let go of the other,*
> *because the one who fears God will be able to avoid*
> *both extremes. (Ecclesiastes 7:18 GW)*

This is not an excuse to live according to our personal sense of right and wrong. That would not lead to a life of moderation or stability. Living by our own sense of right and wrong leads to a confused and compromised life. We're advised to avoid extremes. Either an extreme pursuit of righteousness or giving ourselves over to wickedness. The key to doing this is fearing God.

existential reflections for everyday life

I know good people, decent people with high character values. I enjoy being with them. They personify the beneficial wisdom written in the book of Proverbs. But people devoted to their own righteousness are unpleasant to be around. Their perception of goodness becomes suffocating. They seem to suck the life out of everything and everyone around them.

And then, some people are dangerous to be around. They are so duplicitous that it's hard to accept anything they say as true. Some of these people appear evil. Their intentions aren't just questionable, but malevolent. There seems to be no good in them. Inherently foolish people are also dangerous. They're fickle and untrustworthy. Whoever is around them needs to be on guard at all times because their foolishness puts others around them at risk.

Do you know anyone who fits the description of these types of people? How is it possible to avoid these extreme traits? As expressed in verse 18, the key to avoiding these extremes is to fear God. The fear of God, as spoken of in the Bible, is not a paralyzing terrible dread of God, but an acknowledgment and respect for who God is. We can find a good understanding of the fear of God in many places throughout the Psalms and the book of Proverbs. Here are some references you can look up for yourself—Psalms 19:9, 111:10; Proverbs 8:13, 9:10, 14:27, and 19:23.

Atheists are a law unto themselves. Their sense of morality is *their* perception of right and wrong. But what is their standard of goodness and righteousness? This is their dilemma.[2] The spiritualist's basis of goodness is their sense of what is true. This is their problem. Their sense of goodness and truth has no stability or depth—it's wispy, like a vapor lost in the universe. Those who trust in religion can become the most dangerous of people. They may appear righteous, but their hearts can be cold, callous, and judgmental. Jesus described such people as "whitewashed tombstones" (Matthew 23:27-28). Be wary of anyone who claims or seems to think they have all the answers! Are you fearful of those who are foolish or evil? Don't be. Here is what Jesus said about that—

> *And do not fear those who kill the body but cannot kill*
> *the soul. But rather fear Him who is able to destroy*
> *both soul and body in hell. (Matthew 10:28 NKJV)*

What are some simple takeaways from all this?

- Don't try so hard to make sense of everything that happens in life. It will elude and exasperate you.
- Don't put all your effort into being good and wise because you'll make yourself and others miserable.
- But don't throw caution to the wind.
- What *can* you do? Trust God the way a young child trusts their parents.

Trust the Lord in all you do and encounter throughout each day—especially with what is beyond your control and understanding (see Proverbs 3:5-6 GW).

18 /
schemes, snares, and the futility of personal goodness

Certainly, there is no one so righteous on earth that he always does what is good and never sins.

"I have found only this: God made people decent, but they looked for many ways *to avoid being decent*." (Ecclesiastes 7:20, 29 GW)

[context– Ecclesiastes 7:19-29 GW]

---

the good-person syndrome

"I'm a good person." As a pastor, I've heard this statement countless times. Many times, it's offered as a defense in answer to some flawed moral choice or circumstance in a person's life. Let's call it the "good-person syndrome." Even when we know we're in the wrong about something, we don't want to be defined by our moral failure. We may admit to a particular lie or misbehavior yet claim it's not normal for us—"Yes, I know this is wrong but I'm a good person." When I hear people say, "but I'm a good person," it sounds like they're trying to convince themselves more than anyone else.

I believe most of us value morality, ethics, and good behavior. Many people believe in the innate goodness of humanity. Sure, we know there are sociopaths and evil people, but we see them as the exception, not the rule. Even among those in the Christian faith, different opinions abound regarding personal goodness. The spectrum includes those who see people as good, to those who say all humanity is morally bankrupt and depraved.

I've always had difficulty accepting either of these extremes. It's not that I believe in some notion of a balance between the two. I believe it's not an either-or proposition. Every person has the imprint of our Creator, yet we are not intrinsically good on our own.[1] Somehow, I sensed this from childhood but couldn't give a reason for it until much later in life. I know we are all selfish by nature, yet we are not beyond redemption. But Solomon has another thought on all of this in this last segment of chapter seven of Ecclesiastes.

insights

As with the proverbial sayings Solomon collected and wrote in the book of Proverbs, his thoughts in Ecclesiastes need to be understood within their cultural and historical context. This is ancient wisdom, not modern philosophy. Solomon himself is an important part of the context of Ecclesiastes. He excelled in many things, including wisdom, but he also excelled in pursuing excess, especially pleasure and women (Ecclesiastes 2:3-11).

Solomon reminds us of the value of wisdom—it's stronger than ten rulers of a city (Ecclesiastes 7:19). True wisdom—godly wisdom—is better than the combined efforts of human politics and thinking. A simple observation followed this about people—none of us are righteous in and of ourselves (Psalms 14:1-3; Romans 3:10-12). We're given an example of our shortcomings and warned not to take to heart what others say to us or about us. After all, we've all said things about others that are better left unsaid. Our tendency is to say things at an emotional moment and to generalize and objectify others—"They/he always... they/she never... they're all the same like that."

Solomon returns to the nature of wisdom and admits it is too deep to fathom or understand all there is to know. It is beyond human capabilities, and yet, our pride leads us to believe and behave as if we know it all. Even though Solomon sought wisdom with great diligence, he realizes it was beyond his grasp—

> *"I am still seeking a reason for things, but have not found any." (Ecclesiastes 7:28 GW)*

Along the way, Solomon realized the dangers of lust and pleasure. What he says about women (verses 26, 28) comes from his experience with many concubines and wives who turned his heart from the Lord (1 Kings 11:4). This leads us to Solomon's last thought in chapter seven (verse 29 NKJV and GW)—

> *"Truly, this only I have found: That God made man upright, But they have sought out many schemes."*
> *"... God made people decent, but they looked for many ways to avoid being decent."*

Did God really make people "upright"? If so, why do we seek "many schemes (ways) to avoid being decent"?

existential reflections for everyday life

God created people in His image (imago dei–Genesis 1:26-27).[2] We have the spiritual imprint of our Creator embedded in us. We are more than the elements of our DNA—our personal genetic code. This spiritual imprint is the seed of our conscience (Proverbs 20:27; Romans 2:14-15). Spiritual rebirth is the regeneration of this spiritual imprint of God embedded in all humans (John 3:3-8; Titus 3:5). But our conscience gets buried under the thick skin of our innate selfishness, which we inherited from our first ancestors who ate from the tree of the knowledge of good and evil.

If we don't keep our selfish nature in check, our conscience can get numbed and calloused (Ephesians 4:17-19; 1 Timothy 4:2; Titus

1:15). But our natural inclination toward selfishness creates a constant inner conflict. This conflict between our conscience and our selfish inclination is the reason we come up with "schemes" contrary to godly wisdom and sound judgment, as Solomon put it in verse 29 (see above). How can we resolve or overcome this inner conflict? First, we need to acknowledge and admit our human limitations, as Solomon pointed out in verse 24—

> *Whatever wisdom may be, it is out of reach. It is deep,*
> *very deep. Who can find out what it is?*

Here is where we need the Lord's help and guidance. Just as a young child depends on their parents (or grandparents) for help and guidance, so we need God's help. Our youngest grandchildren are learning to put puzzles together. When our grandson was two-years-old, he liked to dump the puzzle pieces out of the box, while his three-year-old sister could fit together the pieces of some puzzles by herself. Of course, this was a learning process they both needed help with. Now, our grandson's big sister helps her brother work on puzzles and we help when he gets too frustrated for her to help him.

Trying to live each day with a clear conscience can frustrate anyone and even lead to a spiraling depression when our frustration goes unchecked. For example, trying to maintain a healthy regimen of diet and exercise can get disrupted easily by the reality of everyday life, especially within a typical family household. I think Solomon gives us a good starting place to help overcome this inner conflict when he says—

> *Don't take everything that people say to heart, or you may*
> *hear your own servant cursing you. Your conscience*
> *knows that you have cursed others many times. (Eccle-*
> *siastes 7:21-22 GW)*

Don't take offense easily or be overly sensitive about what others may say and how they might act. We are our own worst enemies in this. We allow what others say to have too much influence and power over our lives. Not doing this requires us to choose what we dwell on in our minds and how we allow others to affect our emotions.

Just as when our grandchildren get frustrated, overtired, or obstinate, Susan and I need to help them get past their struggles and navigate their way beyond the immediate situation causing the problems. Sometimes we need to employ a "timeout" for them. So it is with us and the Lord. When we get to a point of frustration or anger or perhaps slip into depression, we need to seek the Lord's help, along with the help of others whom we trust.

Sometimes, we need a timeout of sorts. We need to disengage from self-destructive behaviors and the influence of others who feed or stir up our tendency towards self-pity. But we can't stay in a suspended state of not doing anything. Nature hates a vacuum![3] We need to fill our minds with the truth and set our hearts on what is encouraging and uplifting.

But how can we do this?!

- Start by turning off the continuous cycle of "breaking news" and stop scrolling through social media.
- Instead, watch or read something humorous and encouraging.
- Go take a walk or get outside for some fresh air or do something creative.
- Also, fill your mind with the truth of God's Word and your heart with praise and worship (Colossians 3:15-17).

These are some ways to avoid the various schemes and snares of life and the futility of trying to "be a good person."

Seek the goodness of God for your life each day as you seek the truth with a thankful heart.

study questions for ecclesiastes chapter 7

For a more thorough study, read through Ecclesiastes Chapter 7 again to consider and answer the following questions, broken into 3 sections—

Questions for Chapter 7:1-10—

1. What things are deemed "better" than their counterparts?
2. How could sorrow be better than laughter, or going to a funeral rather than a banquet?
3. Why would it be better to hear a wise reprimand than to hear someone praise you?
4. How are we warned about selective memory?
5. Do you allow yourself time to reflect on what and who is important to your life?
6. Do you have people in your life who will be honest with you, and even rebuke you when needed?
7. What do you have a hard time letting go of? Does this dominate your thinking?
8. How can a person keep a good perspective in life, rather than fall into nostalgia or regret?

For Chapter 7:11-18—

1. What are we told about wisdom? Why is it valuable?
2. In what way do good and bad experiences keep us from predicting the future?
3. What are we told about the righteous and the wicked? Does this seem unfair to you?
4. What would help us avoid being too virtuous or too wicked? How does this help?
5. Does your life seem like a treadmill or rollercoaster? If so, have you discovered why this is?
6. How do you handle the difficulties and trials of life?
7. How much does it bother you when things don't go as planned?
8. Are you bothered when some people seem to get away with wrongdoing, while others suffer who seem innocent and good?
9. What's your understanding of the fear of God? Does God fill your heart with awe and wonder?

For Chapter 7:19-29—

1. What are we told about people and the value of wisdom?
2. What advice does Solomon give about listening to what people say about you, and what is the basis for this advice?
3. What did King Solomon find out in his search for wisdom and the reason for life itself?
4. What was Solomon still looking for and what did he learn about God and people?
5. What are your views of human nature, God, and goodness? What do you base this on?
6. If you've been living for a while, how has your view of life and human nature changed?
7. What areas in life are you still seeking answers to?
8. What are you sure about and why?
9. Where do you seek wisdom? How has the wisdom you've gained in life helped you?

19 /
how to discern the times instead of worrying about the future

The mind of a wise person will know the right time and the right way *to act*. There is a right time and a right way *to act* in every situation. Yet, a terrible human tragedy hangs over people. They don't know what the future will bring. So who can tell them how things will turn out? (Ecclesiastes 8:5-7 GW)

[context– Ecclesiastes 8:1-8 GW]

focused on the future

I became a follower of Jesus during the early Jesus People Movement. Much of that time's teaching and evangelistic thrust emphasized the return of the Lord. Books focusing on the second coming of the Lord flooded bookstores then. Although the Lord declared no one could know when He would return (Matthew 24:36; Acts 1:7), it didn't deter many from trying to predict it. And guess what? They were all wrong.

A lot of those books published on end times in the 1970s and 1980s are out of print for good reason. Their predictions were wrong. And yet, many people persist in trying to predict the future of the Lord's coming or the end of the world. But it's a fool's errand.

I suppose we all want to know what the future holds before it comes. This intensifies at the end of each year while looking ahead to the next, especially after 2020. What a tumultuous year! The year 2020 created more questions than answers for what to expect in the coming year. The next year brought renewed hope regarding the impact and restrictiveness of the pandemic, but it also brought many other problems.

As with everyone else, the pandemic disrupted our lives. I canceled travel plans to Peru and an annual pastor's conference because of a severe case of pneumonia. Had I pushed ahead with my plans against medical advice, I'd have been stuck in Peru for weeks because of border closures. We joined millions of other believers who stayed home to watch online services as we waited for the end of the pandemic. It didn't end quickly. Almost two years into it, we still faced restrictions. To say it's been a tumultuous time is a colossal understatement. The number of lives lost and the unbearable grief of families was devastating. Our economy almost came to a standstill. The ripple effect of closed businesses and lost jobs continues. The confusion and polarization over masks, immunity, vaccines and mandates linger, and wondering when things will return to some type of livable normal.

Wanting to know the future isn't new. Far from it! Fortune tellers, seers, and astrological forecasting have been around since ancient times. But our desire to know what will happen next and our fascination with the future can blind us from discerning the present times. When we're so focused on what might happen or could take place, we fail to realize what is going on right now. We find little appreciation or contentment with what is good in the present when we are so invested in how things could be better. This isn't so much an issue of being content or mindful, though both are beneficial. It's about control. We want to determine the outcome of our lives and the world around us, which inevitably includes the lives of others, especially in our immediate sphere of influence. We want to be like God (Genesis 3:4-7).

Growing old with lots of life experience doesn't always translate into wisdom. Longevity is no guarantee of serenity. If a person hasn't learned to trust God for the future, then anxieties, questions, and worry will fill their lives until the end of their days on earth. Real wisdom enables a person to discern the present as it is and lets the future be its own mystery.

insights

Mysteries are revealed over time or at certain points in time. As time passes, the future reveals its mysteries. But not everyone understands the significance of what becomes known. During the Civil War, when the future of our nation was dark and unclear, President Lincoln understood there was more at stake in preserving the union than slavery. And yet, we still grapple with the outcome of the Civil War in various ways.

In these few verses at the beginning of chapter eight, Solomon distinguishes between knowledge and genuine wisdom. The truly wise person can explain things that are a mystery to others, and that wisdom is beneficial and practical. First, it changes a person's countenance—their face shines and softens. They don't look stressed out.

> *Who is really wise? Who knows how to explain things?*
> *Wisdom makes one's face shine, and it changes one's*
> *grim look. (Ecclesiastes 8:1 GW)*

Wisdom helps people understand the past and what is present, and face the future with confidence that what is unknown will become known and understandable. Wisdom can also be practical as discernment—the ability to understand something beyond the appearance of a situation or what lies below the surface. What Solomon says about the king and his power doesn't seem very relevant to many of us in today's world, although some nations have tyrannical leaders (Ecclesiastes 8:3-6 GW).

However, we can draw some practical and relevant points from these verses if we view "the king" as a person of authority, even a boss, especially someone who is authoritarian or seems tyrannical in their attitude and behavior. More than a few of us have worked under leaders who were difficult to tolerate or had a parent who was a strict authoritarian. Perhaps we have been that person in the lives of others.

Here are some simple, practical takeaways.

- Keep your commitments.
- Don't overreact to people, conditions, or situations you have no control over.
- Be discerning rather than judgmental.
- A wise, thought-out response is much wiser than an emotionally driven reaction.
- Reactions in a heated or stressful moment are often unwise and counterproductive.
- Discerning people know and understand the right thing to do at the appropriate or right time.

Here are a couple more thoughts. Worrying about the future is a burden we don't need to carry or struggle with each day. We all have limitations, especially with our number of days on earth *under the sun.* If nothing else, the worldwide Covid-19 pandemic should remind us of how fragile and precious life is. We may not know the number of our days, but we ought to know that wisdom is more beneficial to our lives than living a careless, unrestrained life.

existential reflections for everyday life

Solomon often contrasts wisdom with foolishness and wickedness in the book of Proverbs, as he does here in Ecclesiastes. In this sense, wisdom isn't mere knowledge. We relate sound wisdom to ethics, morality, virtues, integrity of character, and discernment. This kind of wisdom is more spiritual than philosophical. External circumstances or emotions do not drive a person with this kind of wisdom. They're guided by their conscience, grounded in truth. It is godly wisdom. As the apostle James points out, godly wisdom is—

> *... first of all pure; then peace-loving, considerate, submissive, full of mercy and good fruit, impartial and sincere. (James 3:17 NIV)*

Because of these qualities, a person filled with this wisdom understands the importance and value of keeping commitments to others. They're not overreactive or rude, but considerate and sincere. And they don't make hasty decisions or take up their own cause in a rebellious or selfish way. Our nation and the world would benefit from such wisdom in our current culture and political environment. This is also true within many homes and among extended family. This peace-loving, gentle, and sincere wisdom will go a long way to healing and restoring relationships. It can even prevent divisiveness and strife.

The wise person, as described here by Solomon, would discern the times. They wouldn't make rash judgments about people or the events and situations others are involved in. A discerning person will assess what they hear and see instead of making assumptions or impulsive decisions. They neither react nor overreact, but they understand the seasons of life and the nature of cultural changes. When they see changes in their culture, they're not quick to embrace them nor get caught up fighting against what they can't control.

Tough seasons in life don't overcome a discerning person. They aren't in a state of denial or self-absorbed with more pleasant times, as if they'll never end. A person with godly wisdom understands that fate doesn't determine their destiny, nor control everything in their life. They realize the best way to prepare for and accept the end of their life is to commit their life to the One who gave them life.

How can you gain this godly wisdom?

- Seek out and spend time with people who have godly wisdom, as James describes above.

- Be grounded in the truth of God—His Word—the Bible.
- Listen for the voice of God's Spirit and pay attention to your conscience.

Think about these things and consider what else you might need to do to gain godly wisdom. It will help you discern the times.

20 /
enigmas, the fear of god, and a shadowy life

A sinner may commit a hundred crimes and yet live a long life. Still, I know with certainty that it will go well for those who fear God, because they fear him. But it will not go well for the wicked... Their lives are like shadows, because they don't fear God. (Ecclesiastes 8:12-13 GW)

[context– Ecclesiastes 8:9-13 GW]

---

the enigmas of life

My wife loves to watch a good mystery movie or series. I'm sure many people do. I do too, but I like variety. There are mysteries in life that engage me as much as a good story, but not mysteries with an unsolved crime. Those can catch my attention for a while, but there are more puzzling situations in life that are harder to comprehend. I find plenty of them in the Bible. Such things cause some people to discount the Bible as a reliable source of truth, so they reject it. I find the Bible's honesty to be refreshing and its enigmas intriguing.

What's unknown or yet to be revealed intrigues us. Whether fiction or nonfiction, mysteries engage our curiosity, hold our interest, and require us to think. But some mysteries in life are enigmas to us.[1] These puzzling dilemmas mystify and frustrate us. This includes situations beyond our grasp or that defy reason and understanding. This seems to be the impetus for Solomon's writings in Ecclesiastes. He alludes to some enigmatic topics in the book of Proverbs, but in Ecclesiastes, Solomon seems to do a deep dive into these enigmas in life. Such things prompt hard questions. Why do bad things happen to good people? Why do some people seem to get away with wrongdoing over and over?

This list could go on and on with questions that have no easy or satisfying answers. These types of questions often lead to two different outcomes or reactions—whining or worship. By whining, I mean a sense of frustration that can boil into volcanic anger and rage or spiral into a deep depression. Worship lifts us up to focus on the One who knows the answers to all our why questions, even though He may not give us the answers we want or when we want them.

Although God often gets blamed for what goes wrong in the world or in a person's life, God is not the one who brings the complications. We only have ourselves to blame. The complex layers of mysteries in this *life under the sun* result from billions of people going their own way for millennia. Each person exercises their free will, even at the expense of others and themselves.

insights

Solomon was the king of Israel, a nation that was to be governed by the Covenant Law given through Moses. Within the Law of the Covenant, we find what's called the Law of Retribution, where we get the phrases, *an eye for an eye, tooth for a tooth*, and similar laws.[2] These laws prevented revenge and provided fair but limited justice.

The covenant between God and the people of Israel was a binding relationship based on the people of Israel accepting these laws and their impact on their relationships with one another. But Israel was not faithful to this covenant relationship, as the biblical history of Israel reveals. They were unfaithful to God even though He was faithful to them. Justice, as prescribed in the Mosaic Law, was often neglected and violated. This unfaithfulness had a ripple effect upon them as a nation and on their relationships with one another.

Although Solomon knew of Israel's unfaithful history, he also knew the promises God made to Israel, and he knew God's faithfulness. He also knew of the great promise made to his father, King David, which we know as a Messianic promise (2 Samuel 7:16).[3] This is the background and frame of reference we need to keep in mind as we read these few verses in chapter eight filled with enigmas. Verse 9 is a bridge or transition from the previous verses.

Solomon understood the consequences of a person in authority using their power to abuse or oppress others. There is not only the ultimate justice God would bring upon them but also the effects on those who abuse their authority. As the popular saying goes, "power tends to corrupt and absolute power corrupts absolutely."[4] When anyone has authority over others, if the authority is unchecked, it will corrupt the behavior and character of the person who holds such power. This includes employers, church leaders, and parents.

A key to understanding Solomon's perspective is the fear of God. We need to be clear about how different the fear of the Lord is from the state of fear itself. Solomon's father, King David, gives some insight into what the fear of the Lord looks like—

> *Come, you children, listen to me; I will teach you the fear*
> *of the Lord… Keep your tongue from evil, And your*
> *lips from speaking deceit. Depart from evil and do*
> *good; Seek peace and pursue it. (Psalms 34:11, 13-14*
> *NKJV)*

This is similar to what Solomon penned in Proverbs as personified through the voice of Godly Wisdom—

> *To fear the Lord is to hate evil; I hate pride and arro-*

> *gance, evil behavior and perverse speech. (Proverbs*
> *8:13 NIV)*

Understanding the purpose and value of fearing the Lord helps us better understand Solomon's observations and conclusions. Yes, some people have a veneer of spirituality but are flawed in character and known for wickedness, and though known for their wickedness, people laud them at their funerals as if they were good. And yes, even when someone seems to get away with evil "a hundred times," the Lord doesn't overlook it. And it won't benefit them because "their lives are like shadows."

This is the consequence when a person commits a crime with no accountability. Plenty of examples exist of people who avoid prison because of legal mistakes and technicalities, or partiality by judges and juries. But Solomon brings us back to a simple conclusion and outlook on life—

Fearing the Lord is still a beneficial and wise way of life.

existential reflections for everyday life

When we have a genuine fear of God, it motivates us to live in a way that benefits us and others in the long run. We understand God will hold every person accountable for their life—both those who are good and bad. With this assurance in our hearts, our minds are able and free to accept that some dark and mysterious situations in life will continue to be mysteries. When we see wrongs that aren't made right, we can choose to be frustrated and filled with strife or choose to entrust such things to the Lord. If the Lord makes it clear you should right a wrong, then do so. But if He doesn't, don't go chasing causes for your own sense of rightness.

In our ministry to abandoned and abused children and young women, we did what we could for those God entrusted to us.[5] But what we did through our ministry was small compared to the need throughout the world. Others suggested we should do more or pursue other causes.

But we understood our responsibility was to the Lord and what He gave us to do, not what others expected of us.

Because I fear the Lord, I'm grieved by evil and wickedness when I hear of it or see it. But so much of it is beyond my capability or understanding, so I entrust such things to the Lord. Some situations in life and the world at large are still enigmas to me. I can neither accept nor explain them. These dark mysteries of *life under the sun* are just that— puzzling, dark enigmas. I look forward to the day when the Lord shines His righteous light on these enigmas and resolves them. The apostle Paul reminds us—

> *For now we see only a reflection as in a mirror; then we shall see face to face. Now I know in part; then I shall know fully, even as I am fully known. (1 Corinthians 13:12 NIV)*

Are you living a life in the shadows or in the light?

In the fear of God or in ignorance?

I choose to walk in the light of God.

21 /
enjoying life is biblical and recommended

So I recommend the enjoyment of life. People have nothing better to do *under the sun* than to eat, drink, and enjoy themselves. This joy will stay with them while they work hard during their brief lives which God has given them *under the sun*. (Ecclesiastes 8:15 GW)

[context– Ecclesiastes 8:14-17 GW]

our frustrations in life

My wife and I grew up with very different family experiences—almost polar opposites. It was as if we grew up in two different countries from one another. You could say we grew up in two different family cultures, for sure. Susan's family showed little outward affection, while my folks and I effused affection in private and public view. My family talked about everything in long-winded dinner discussions. Susan's family hardly talked at meals or otherwise. I received supportive encouragement with a permissive mindset. But our family values were not clear. My wife grew up in a strict, disciplinarian home with clearly defined roles for her brothers, her sister, and herself.

When we began our relationship, and in the early years of our marriage, our expectations were wildly different. It took time and much effort to reframe our lives with more realistic and reasonable expectations than we had at the beginning of our life together.

Depending on our level of tolerance, the amount of frustration we experience in life depends on how well we manage our expectations or if we allow them to manage us. We all get frustrated with circumstances, life situations, and people. But our frustrations are of our own making because of the expectations we have of people and events in life. This becomes clear when saying things like, "I just don't understand why *they* insist on doing (or not doing) [such-and-such]." Or "Why is this allowed to continue?" or "How could this happen?" Statements and questions like these imply unmet expectations. When something doesn't sit right with us, we question or challenge it. We usually base our expectations in life or of people on our experiences in childhood and how we think things should or should not be.[1]

Have you ever noticed how people who seem easygoing also seem to enjoy life? Perhaps you're one of those people. If not, you either envy them or resent them. Why? Because of your expectations. Can how we handle or manage our expectations determine whether we are a person who sees the glass as half-full or half-empty? Perhaps. Can we change how we manage our expectations? I believe so. Can we influence others, or can they influence us to better manage our expectations? Yes! I know this from experience—my wife's influence on me.

Why is it important to learn how to manage our expectations? Our enjoyment of life is most often related to how well we manage our expectations. Consider Solomon's observations and conclusions made at the end of chapter eight.

insights

These last few verses in Ecclesiastes eight repeat and reinforce Solomon's earlier existential reflections. This isn't Solomon thinking in circles, as if he's forgotten what he said before. It's intentional. It's like saying, "Don't get lost or caught up in what you don't understand." In verse 14, Solomon observes what we might call the inverse of the law of retribution or the inverse of the law of sowing and reaping. It is the exact opposite of what we expect or want. This prompts questions like —"Why do bad things happen to good people?" Solomon points out that we might say—"It's just not fair!" He sees this as another "point-less" reality of *life under the sun*. This is familiar to Solomon's thought in Ecclesiastes 3:16, which reminds us of the existence of evil. It's a reality. Something we can neither erase nor resolve.

After this observation, Solomon returns to a thought he introduced earlier (Ecclesiastes 2:24-25; 3:12-13; 5:18-20). Verse 15 gets misunderstood or misconstrued often, especially the phrase, "*... eat, drink, and be merry" (Ecclesiastes 3:15 NKJV)*. It gets distorted as a misrepresented version of Epicurean philosophy.[2] The apostle Paul addresses this (in 1 Corinthians 15:32) and Jesus alludes to it also (Luke 12:19). This is not an encouragement by Solomon to *party on* and forget about everything else. Solomon speaks from a worldly view of life, but this also needs to be understood within its context here and the intended purpose for the writing of Ecclesiastes (see Ecclesiastes 12:13-14 GW).

First, keep in mind the other thought Solomon reiterates—pursuing wisdom as an end-all-be-all answer will not resolve all of life's mysteries (verses 16-17). All that God does is beyond our grasp. Even for those who claim to have all the answers. This final thought in chapter eight reaches back to chapter three, where Solomon declares all things in life have a time and purpose, but the future is beyond our capacity to know. Therefore, Solomon encourages us to enjoy our life the best we can because it's the means God gave us to endure the work given to us. It is a way to manage our expectations in life and not become overly frustrated with *life under the sun*.

existential reflections for everyday life

We express a popular adage of our day in various ways, but here it is in a nutshell — "*Don't worry about what you can't control, focus on what you can control.*" Even this sentiment may be more than a person can handle at certain points in their life. I prefer the simplicity and beauty of the summary of the Serenity Prayer by Reinhold Niebuhr embedded in the philosophy of Alcoholics Anonymous—[3]

> "God grant us the serenity to accept the things we cannot change, courage to change the things we can, and wisdom to know the difference."

Things beyond our control only have power over us because of our expectations about them. Yes, of course, some circumstances, life situations, and even some people may exert power over us in some way. But their power is not supreme nor sovereign—only God is sovereign over all.

Many unexpected and unwanted disappointments filled the year 2020 with frustrations, hardships, and tragedies. And that's an understatement for many of us. But one year is not forever. There have been much darker times in world history. However—we only know for sure what we experience ourselves. When we manage our expectations, we can exert a sense of control over what is beyond our control. Think about your expectations. We can be like a child at Christmas time with a wishlist that exceeds reality, but this will set us up for great disappointments and frustrations.

How can we better handle whatever is to come in the future? We can choose to appreciate and value what we have in our lives rather than what we don't. It's not just a "count your blessings" mindset, but a choice to not dwell on our disappointments. Most, if not all, disappointments result from unmet expectations. And most of those unmet expectations come from misplaced trust. It is a given that people will disappoint us sooner or later. We all disappoint others and they let us down.

If none of us knows the future—and none of us do—then we need to live our lives more in the present. I'm not speaking of mindfulness, although that may be helpful too. Many of our expectations are either unrealistic or unreasonable or both. I believe this is what Solomon intends when he says—

> *So I recommend the enjoyment of life. People have nothing*
> *better to do* under the sun *than to eat, drink, and*
> *enjoy themselves. This joy will stay with them while*
> *they work hard during their brief lives which God has*
> *given them* under the sun. *(Ecclesiastes 8:15 GW)*

Simple enjoyment of life is a gift from God to help us endure *life under the sun*. This isn't wishful thinking or a denial of reality. Having lived overseas for many years and traveling to some remote areas in Southeast Asia, Ethiopia, and the South Pacific, I've witnessed people who have learned to find simple enjoyment in their lives. It is easy for someone like me from a more prosperous nation to focus on what people don't have in less prosperous nations. While overseas, I heard many American visitors say, "These people seem to be so joyful with so little in life." Exactly! But you don't have to travel to a remote village somewhere to learn this. When you learn to find joy in life instead of longing for more of what others have, it will eliminate many frustrations.

> *Do you see what is good in your life or dwell on your disappointments?*

> *Do endless frustrations seem to haunt you, or can you let go of unrealistic and unreasonable expectations?*

It's your choice each day.

I choose to enjoy life as a gift from God every day.

study questions for ecclesiastes chapter 8

For a more thorough study, read through Ecclesiastes Chapter 8 again to consider and answer the following questions broken into 2 sections—

Questions for Chapter 8:1-10—

1. What is said about wisdom and those with wisdom?
2. What advice does Solomon give regarding the king's commands (re: governing laws)?
3. What is said about the timing of what to say and what to do? What will we not know?
4. What do we not have power over? Why?
5. What else doesn't seem to make sense to Solomon?
6. In what ways have you gained wisdom beyond knowledge?
7. What is your experience of compliance with the government or with civil disobedience?
8. Is it easy or difficult for you to manage your time well?
9. What do you think helps or hinders you with your time management?
10. How do you cope with injustice and wrong in this life?
11. Do you trust God with your time and your future?

———

For Chapter 8:11-17—

1. What seems to be the result when there are no consequences for committing a crime?
2. What is said to be the benefit for those who fear God over those who don't?
3. What does Solomon recommend as a break from hard work? Do you agree with this? Why or why not?
4. What will remain beyond the understanding of the wisest people? Why?
5. How do you view injustices in the world?
6. Do you see injustices as humanity's problem or God's neglect or indifference?
7. Have you ever suffered wrong or injustice? If so, how did you handle it?
8. Are you able to disengage from work and the problems of the world to enjoy life?
9. When you can't understand things in life, are you able to trust these things to God?

22 /
the equality of death and hope for the living

Now, I have carefully thought about all this, and I explain it in this way: Righteous people and wise people, along with their accomplishments, are in God's hands...

This is the tragedy of everything that happens under the sun: Everyone shares the same destiny... But all who are among the living have hope... (Ecclesiastes 9:1, 3-4 GW)

[context– Ecclesiastes 9:1-6 GW]

---

when hope seems limited

My mom passed away in October 2019. I'm thankful for the timing of her death. It was just before the pandemic reared its ugly head in our nation. How could I be thankful for this? My mom was in the memory care wing of an assisted living facility near our home. It was so close I would sometimes ride my bike over to see her. I got to know the staff pretty well, and they seemed to enjoy caring for her. But government-mandated restrictions changed all of that.

I didn't have to go through the frustration of not being able to visit her in person—the experience for many families during the height of the pandemic. Even when they were dying, family members could not say their goodbyes to their parents, grandparents, or extended family members. This struck home for me when my doctor related his frustrations with not being able to visit his parents in another upscale assisted living facility. Even though he was a doctor and understood how to follow the precautions to not spread Covid-19, he couldn't visit them. He watched his parents' lives slowly wither away but was helpless to care for them. His sadness was palpable. I'm thankful I didn't endure the same sad end of life with my mom's passing.

We all remember the feelings we experience during tragic events. I remember how difficult it was to hear of the thousands of people who died as a result of Covid-19. A shadow of death seemed to hang over the world like a heavy blanket. It dampened hope and closed us in. When circumstances beyond our control limit our hope, life seems bleak. It wasn't just the fear of death, but the realness of its finality. Many of us felt confined by an invisible enemy. Confined physically because of confusion, fear, and politics. The challenges and conditions experienced in 2020 were not new. History is replete with famines, plagues, natural disasters, and an abundance of man-made calamities and wars. Considering all that *could* go wrong in the world, life can seem grim. But is it? Is that just the reality of *life under the sun*?

During the confusing and confounding events of the pandemic of 2020, a major debilitating factor wasn't the disease itself but the impact of isolation and lockdowns. Public health policies and protocols seemed draconian in many states. The general effect of *social distancing* was crippling isolation from others—among friends, families, and within communities. People felt cut off from one another. A sense of normalcy in life was missing, but the public was told to embrace this as a "new normal." The heartbeat of communities at all levels, big or small, grew weaker by the month. The economy around the world floundered and created great stress for individuals, families, businesses, and entire nations. Lockdowns resulted in an economic meltdown. Although it was an artificially induced economic recession, the stress from it was real and debilitating. How does one make sense of such things?

What makes life less than grim and even enjoyable?

insights

As said in various ways—*death is the great equalizer.*[1] This is Solomon's summarizing thought in verse 2—

> *All things come alike to all: One event happens to the*
> *righteous and the wicked; (Ecclesiastes 9:2 NKJV).*

Death is no respecter of persons. God determined this after sin entered the world (Genesis 2:7; 3:19). Man—formed and composed of the elements of the earth—became a living soul when God breathed life into him. But the impact of sin—the selfish predisposition in all of us —introduced physical death into the world. It doesn't matter what we have done in life or when death comes. Death brings a certain equality. This is Solomon's main point here.

However, the leveling effect of sin is all we see when our only perspective is *life under the sun.* This, *under the sun* life perspective, is what Solomon reiterates often (Ecclesiastes 2:14-16; 3:19-20; 6:6; 7:2). Why does Solomon return to this lament repeatedly? He does so to remind us of the value and importance of living while we are alive and explains this with some proverbial wisdom in verses 4-6. I see this as a glimmer of light in the darkness of *life under the sun.* It was not a new thought then, nor is it now. Life precedes death, so enjoy it. Value life itself while you can.

In the first three verses of chapter nine, Solomon puts forth his typical fatalistic view of life. It doesn't matter who you are or aren't, what you do or don't do, we all die. But in verse 4, Solomon shines a glimmer of light into all of this dark destiny—

> *But all who are among the living have hope, because a*
> *living dog is better than a dead lion. (GW)*

Solomon uses some obvious contrasts to underscore his point of living your life while you can. He doesn't give more insight on this, but his point is—while a person is alive, they have hope. Many philosophers and psychologists, whether atheist or agnostic, say when a person draws their last breath and their heart stops—that's it—fade-to-black. But is there more? I believe so, and Solomon seems to have a similar hope. What did Solomon have in mind about hope?

existential reflections for everyday life

The concept of an afterlife or existence beyond physical death pre-dates both Judaism and Christianity in more ancient religions.[2] Belief in a resurrection from the dead for Christian believers is a cornerstone of Christian theology (1 Corinthians 15:13-17). Jesus personified this belief in a literal sense. He declared it before and after His death (John 11:25; Luke 24). Solomon would not understand physical resurrection as Christian believers do now, but he had some sense of resurrection or life after death from all his studies of wisdom.

Although Solomon's focus in Ecclesiastes is on *life under the sun*, he speaks of hope in this life while alive. Why does Solomon speak of hope after all the pessimistic reflections so far? What would spark this sense of hope? Solomon holds a belief almost every one of us has. Most people believe there must be more than mere existence on earth, something beyond the physical existence of all that is observable in the universe.

The natural world reveals a sense of design and purpose with its various cycles and seasons observed each day and year by year. It illustrates a continuity of life. One psalm written by King David, Solomon's father, reminds us of these natural cycles and seasons and how they reveal the glory of God as Creator of all life (Psalms 19:1-4). Hope is a belief that transcends the immediate concerns of life. Hope is a way of seeing beyond the limitations of *life under the sun*. Trust is the anchor of genuine hope—trust in the Creator and Sustainer of all life. Hope helps us make sense of *life under the sun*.

Even our memories of what is good and enjoyable in life help propel us from one day to the next. Recovering from and overcoming difficulties experienced in times past instills a sense of hope for life today and the days beyond. When we value our relationships with family and friends, we gain hope. We can see a greater purpose in life because of the benefit of our interdependence upon one another.

In the 1950s, Americans worked hard to rebuild the economy and gain a better life in the aftermath of WWII. But a realization dawned in the chaos and upheaval of the '60s for the need to appreciate the simple things in life. Perhaps the two songs—*Cat's in the Cradle* and *Stop and Smell the Roses*—express the sentiment of valuing people and appreciating the simple life.[3]

We all benefit from enjoying the simple blessings in our life like food, shelter, safety, breath, and health. Finding enjoyment in life isn't about pleasure—it's an appreciation for life itself. When we appreciate life itself, it becomes a basis for hope. This simple sense of hope sustains us each day. As Solomon said, *"a living dog is better than a dead lion"* (verse 4). No matter how basic and simple our life may seem, it is better than a thousand famous people who are now dead and forgotten.

But those of us who trust in Jesus as Lord have an eternal, living hope because of our assurance in the Lord who conquered death by His resurrection from the dead (1 Peter 1:3). This hope enables us to see *beyond* our life *under the sun*. This hope is more than a sentimental feeling—it is an anchor to our soul (Romans 5:2-5; Hebrews 6:19).

Because I came to faith in Jesus not long before becoming a parent, I was confident of life beyond this life *under the sun*. And as a young dad, I made time to enjoy my family in simple ways with the assurance of eternal life. We can choose to value life daily—even in the darkest times.

There is hope for the living and there is a living hope for those who trust in the Lord—the One who gives us life.

the power of commitment and the burden of potential

Enjoy life with your wife, whom you love, during all your brief, pointless life. God has given you your pointless life under the sun. This is your lot *in life* and what you get for the hard work that you do under the sun. Whatever presents itself for you to do, do it with *all* your might, because there is no work, planning, knowledge, or skill in the grave where you're going. (Ecclesiastes 9:9-10 GW)

[context– Ecclesiastes 9:7-12 GW]

expectations make potential a burden

"She has great potential!" How many times has this been said about someone who never quite lived up to expectations? Probably too often to count. Charles Schulz, the creator of Peanuts, said, "There is no heavier burden than an unfulfilled potential."[1]

I remember being told by my parents and high school guidance counselor that I had great potential but just needed to apply myself more. The guidance counselor told my folks he expected me to "really go places." Well, I *did* travel to many places in the world to do ministry, but I'm pretty sure he had something else in mind. I didn't live up to all those expectations, whatever they were. In fact, I bailed out on them before I graduated high school. But I learned how to enjoy life in a simple way and do a lot of things no one expected of me—including me. Sometimes, I look back with some regret about what I could have or would have done. Then I realize how many great opportunities and blessings I've enjoyed *because* my life didn't follow the course of other people's expectations.

Telling someone they have great potential is like hanging a heavy chain around their neck. It becomes a sentence of vague but overwhelming expectations. How does anyone live up to what is not and cannot be defined? Sadly, the expectation of potential is common in many spheres of life—athleticism, creativity, intelligence, and career opportunities are just a few. When saddled with some vague possibility, how would a person know when they've fulfilled their potential?

I believe the pronouncement of having great potential is a plague in our present culture. Projections and predictions about events, people, and opportunities seem to cement their future as certain. Unfortunately, most of these projections and probabilities doom people to fail because the expectations are far too high and unrealistic. Many college athletes who turn pro are told *the sky's the limit* regarding their career potential. But when they don't become a superstar or accomplish certain milestones, they're deemed a failure. This happens to musicians, politicians, scientists, writers, and other fields or areas of expertise.

insights

Once again, Solomon gives the advice to enjoy life and whatever work we have to do in this *"pointless life under the sun"* (verse 9). At first, it may seem Solomon is encouraging us to set low expectations and settle for whatever comes our way in this *life under the sun* when he says, *"This is your lot in life..."* (verse 9). And yet, what he says after this advice gives a more complete understanding of what may seem simplistic and fatalistic.

The first thing to keep in mind is the immediacy of life, which helps us to live in the present. The problem with expectations and potential is their open-ended dependency on the future—something no one knows for certain. When we value the future over the present, we over-value what could or might be and shortchange what is. Focusing on expectations and potential pushes us into making comparisons, which is a no-win scenario. It's like trying to catch a phantom. Holograms are intriguing and videoconferencing is useful, but you can't hug a holo-gram or a screen image. There is no comparison between what is real and what is virtual. Seeing people in person rather than on a screen is more, well, real.

Here is a simple observation and summary of what Solomon says in verses 10-12—*commit yourself to do your best and don't give much energy or interest to possibilities and personal potential.* The unpredictability of the future and the harsh reality of *life under the sun* are beyond our control. If this sounds like a familiar theme or repeated thought, it is! We all overlook what is basic and obvious in exchange for what is yet to be or could be. But in doing this, we ignore what has a true and known value.

existential reflections for everyday life

The idea of enjoying simple pleasures in life each day reminds us to value life and the people in our lives. Don't focus on what others might have that you don't. Appreciate and value those whom you love and let simple joys in your life fill your heart. This is the meaning behind what Solomon says in verses 7-8—

> *Go, enjoy eating your food, and drink your wine cheer-fully, because God has already accepted what you've done. Always wear clean clothes, and never go without lotion on your head. (Ecclesiastes 9:7-8 GW)*

How does this have any practical value to us? How should we under-stand it? It's not about keeping up appearances but choosing to look good to feel good. There's an adage that if you look good, you'll feel good. But is it true? There are some studies that validate this, but it has more to do with internal perceptions than just outward appearance.[2]

When my mom became a widow in her 80s, she would spend much time and effort putting her makeup on and getting dressed for her daily visit to Starbucks. While there, the servers would dote on her as she read, dozed off, and chatted with others. This was important for her well-being. It was her social life and helped her cope with growing old. If she didn't get ready to go out each day, she was more likely to stay in her PJs and lay in bed depressed about her life.

A simple way to counter the monotony, routine, and sense of pointlessness in life is to look your best and do your best each day. Does it sound too simplistic? Maybe. But simplicity is a way of getting beyond the confusion of what we don't understand and can't control and not getting swept up in that confusion as it swirls around us.

Another dilemma in *life under the sun* is when we lack commitment. Making a commitment to anything (or anyone) requires a person to overcome various hindrances. What hinders you from making or following through on commitments? Here are a few possibilities, perhaps probabilities—fear of failure, fear of the unknown, fear of missing out (FOMO), apathy or indifference, lack of confidence, laziness, negative self-talk, and even arrogance. Whatever the reason, when we're unable or unwilling to commit to doing something or follow through on our commitments, it puts our emotional, mental, and spiritual health at risk. Commitment to move forward frees us from the black hole of what may seem like pointlessness in *life under the sun*. When we accomplish something and follow through on a commitment, we gain a sense of purpose. When we have a sense of purpose in life, it lessens the weight of the expectations of others and lifts the burden of unmeasurable potential.

There may not be any guarantees in this life, but there are some assurances, small mercies, and simple encouragements along the path of a life with purpose. Setting goals, expectations, strategies, and other focuses on the future can impede, overwhelm, and stifle us. When we look too far down the road, we lose sight of what's good all around us.

Often, the best goal is to just do the next thing and the best strategy is to do the next thing well. At the end of any day, with some minor accomplishments, we can experience satisfaction, and enjoy and share this satisfaction with those we love and value. Look your best, do what you can, do it well, and enjoy life as well as you can with those you love and respect.

What expectations can you abandon to make your life simpler?

Don't complicate your life.

Live it with simplicity and purpose.

wisdom is better than strength or weapons of war

So I said, "Wisdom is better than strength," even though that poor person's wisdom was despised, and no one listened to what he said. One should pay more attention to calm words from wise people than shouting from a ruler of fools. Wisdom is better than weapons of war... (Ecclesiastes 9:16-18 GW)

[context– Ecclesiastes 9:13-18 GW]

human nature is remarkably consistent

My wife and I are near polar opposites in personality. I'm more overt and assertive than my wife, and that's putting it mildly. She is innately more gracious and kind toward others than me. I've learned to be more so because of her influence in my life. She's become more assertive in some ways, probably as a means of survival to live with me. In other ways, we balance each other out. I usually enjoy speaking in front of a group of people and meeting new people in various settings. Susan is not comfortable meeting a lot of new people in unfamiliar settings and prefers not to speak in front of people. We're very different and this balancing of one another benefits our marriage. I see this as how two people become one in marriage (Genesis 2:24).

It's not so much a merging of personalities into one, but a sense of wholeness not possible otherwise.

Personalities may vary, yet there is a sameness about them throughout time. In recent times, we can analyze and categorize a person's personality with various personality tests.[1] Although these tests vary in terminology and analysis, they confirm how consistent human nature is. The most consistent element of human nature is our self-centeredness. Personality tests may help determine *how* we are self-centered and to what degree, but all focus on the self in each person. Each one of us cares more about ourselves than any other person does. This is natural. We are born with this self-centered nature. But we're not all selfish in the same way. Some of us prefer others to serve us, which makes us feel better about ourselves. Others feel better when they serve others. Most of us are in the middle of that spectrum.

We all know people who seem to think the universe revolves around them. They have a sense of importance that overshadows others and crowds them out of their lives. They're known as bullies, egomaniacs, narcissists, or megalomaniacs. These people are usually abusive, oppressive, and tyrannical toward others. You probably know people who are the opposite. People who are kind and gracious. They may have an upbeat, sunny disposition or are shy and quiet. They often help others and do what is right and best for all concerned. We all need the latter group of people in our lives and, hopefully, value them for who they are. You might identify with a little of both, but perhaps with the first group more than you realize.

We can become less self-centered when we choose and seek to become more like our Creator. This will take place based on our view of others, ourselves, and God. People are people. We are who we are. But people can change! Wisdom—godly wisdom (James 3:16-17 CSB)—is what can help change our perspective, which is too often clouded by the wisdom of this world. As Solomon points out, there is a wisdom greater than what or who seems most powerful in the world in this *life under the sun.*

insights

Wisdom and sound judgment seldom get the respect they deserve. People who are more concerned with their own importance and input can ignore or undervalue sound reasoning and discernment. This seems to be what makes a "deep impression" on Solomon (Ecclesiastes 9:13 GW). He illustrates this point with a short story about a poor person whose wisdom saved a town from a powerful king, found in verses 13-16.

Whether or not a true event, we don't know. But it confirms and illustrates what holds true in life in two ways. We continue failing to learn from history and we forget good deeds and who performed them. We see examples of this in the lives of Joseph and Daniel—both wise beyond their years and with their goodness forgotten by those who benefited from them. Joseph suffered mistreatment by his brothers, and Potiphar's wife used Joseph's integrity against him (Genesis 37:19-28; 39:11-20). While in prison, Joseph interpreted important dreams for two people, but they forgot his good deeds for two years (Genesis 40:12-23). Daniel interprets dreams for Nebuchadnezzar, the great emperor of Babylon, but other nobles despise him for this. Later, the grandson of Nebuchadnezzar forgets about his wisdom and value as a leader until his services are once again required (Daniel 5:12-29).

We find countless similar examples throughout history. Many inventions and scientific breakthroughs resulted from unintentional discoveries by people now forgotten. Important historical events like World War I took place because of now-forgotten situations and people. Absalom might have captured and killed King David if he followed the advice of his advisor, Ahithophel, which would have changed the course of history and perhaps eternity. Instead, he followed advice from another advisor loyal to David, and Ahithophel killed himself (2 Samuel 17).

Wisdom is powerful, but only when heeded.

existential reflections for everyday life

Knowledge and wisdom are not the same, and godly wisdom is distinct from human wisdom. Wisdom is knowledge with understanding—explainable and useful. Think of knowledge as data for a computer and wisdom as the software that can process the data. Godly wisdom is best described by the apostle James—

> ... *the wisdom that is from above is first pure, then peaceable, gentle, willing to yield, full of mercy and good fruits, without partiality and without hypocrisy.*
> *(James 3:17 NKJV)*

We find intelligence and wisdom in people of all ages, genders, races, and statuses. I found this to be true throughout the many places I've traveled and worked. I've benefitted from the wisdom and insight of many people whom I've worked with, for, and supervised as their leader many times. This helped me appreciate and value the people I had the blessing and privilege of overseeing in many areas of ministry. It also applies to my family. Even my grandchildren remind me of what is good, right, just, wise, and valuable.

It's easy to see the injustice and wrong done to this *"poor, wise person"* (Ecclesiastes 9:15). They benefited from his wisdom, but did not respect him. But that's not what makes a deep impression on Solomon. Here are 3 observations and conclusions made by Solomon—

- *"Wisdom is better than strength"* — Strength and power wane and weaken over time but wisdom does not (verse 16).
- *"Pay more attention to calm words from wise people"* — This aligns with how James described wisdom as *"peaceable, gentle, willing to yield... without partiality... [or] hypocrisy."* (verse 17)
- *"Wisdom is better than weapons of war"* — The *"poor, wise person"* outsmarted the powerful king who surrounded and blockaded the town (verse 18).

Ah, but there's a caveat to all this wisdom — "... *but one sinner can destroy much that is good*" (verse 18). And this brings us back to the primary truth we can observe, understand, and apply in our own lives—

> *One should pay more attention to calm words from wise*
> *people than shouting from a ruler of fools. (Ecclesiastes*
> *9:17 GW)*

Heeding this simple admonition from Solomon would prevent or more easily resolve most conflict and strife, and avert costly and deadly wars. Wise words and a calm spirit are more beneficial and powerful than intellect or authority. Solomon echoes this in his Proverbs (Proverbs 15:18; 16:32; 17:27) and we find the same wisdom in the epistle of James (James 1:19). What stands in the way of this admonition being heeded? The usual things—emotions like fear and pride, power and selfishness.

If you want your life to go well and have a beneficial impact on people and the world around you—choose the way of the *"poor, wise person."*

How?

Pursue godly wisdom that reflects godly character.

study questions for ecclesiastes chapter 9

For a more thorough study, read through Ecclesiastes Chapter 9 again to consider and answer the following questions broken into 2 sections—

Questions for Chapter 9:1-10—

1. How is the state of death a great equalizer of people?
2. Why is death the destiny of all people, whether good or bad?
3. Since death is certain for all, what are we encouraged to do?
4. How are we to go about life's work and for what reason?
5. What do you worry about?
6. Does the thought of death paralyze or motivate you?
7. How do you handle what is beyond your control?
8. Do you obsess over what's beyond your control, ignore it, or see beyond it?
9. Are you thankful for the life you have?
10. Are you able to live above life's difficulties?
11. In what ways have you learned to make the most of your time each day?

For Chapter 9:11-18—

1. What are some things noted as unfair in these verses?

2. What are two things that can happen to anybody over time?
3. What is the injustice done in the story of the wise man and the city?
4. In the face of injustice, what does King Solomon claim is better? Why?
5. When have you seen true injustice? Did you do anything to help resolve it?
6. How have you handled what appears to be unfairness or an unjust situation in your own life?
7. Do you seek ways to move beyond what seems unjust or unfair in life?
8. How do you react when you see injustice?
9. Do you complain about injustice or are you moved with compassion to do something about it?

wisdom prepares the way for success

If an ax is blunt and the edge isn't sharpened, then one has to use more strength. But wisdom prepares the way for success. (Ecclesiastes 10:10 GW)

[context– Ecclesiastes 10:1-10 GW]

---

discernment and discretion

"Lord, help me know what to say to these people!" This is a basic prayer I silently and often prayed as I counseled people in desperate situations. I prayed this while trying to answer people who seemed unable to grasp basic spiritual truths. The truth is—I prayed this simple prayer a lot as a pastor. This was also true when our family moved overseas. We encountered diverse customs and values from our own as we developed and directed two separate ministries for nearly a quarter of a century. This forced us to rethink our previous ministry experience and interactions with people. Our work needed to fit different people from ourselves—a people whose culture and language differed from ours. It also required us to seek the Lord's guidance often. We needed godly discernment and discretion daily.

Discernment and discretion are valuable qualities in everyday life. Here's a simple way to understand the difference between the two. Discernment is an understanding that sees below the appearance of a situation. Discerning people understand the intent and deeper meaning of a person's words. Discretion is the application of discernment. A person with discretion knows how to respond in a given situation or in response to someone's words because they have discernment.

Both discernment and discretion qualify as practical applications or uses of wisdom. Sadly, these valuable applications of wisdom are more scarce than plentiful, much like common sense is not very common. Some might say, "just Google it!" Ah, but the internet is not a reliable source for finding the truth, let alone godly discernment and discretion. Why is there so little common sense or practical wisdom? Perhaps the simplest way to answer this requires an understanding of the powerful influence of foolishness. Foolishness is why things are not always as they appear or the way we think things should be.

Have you heard the term "truth in advertising?" Advertisements and commercials that make far-fetched claims go back to the day of medicine man shows with hucksters who claimed their tonic or snake oil would "cure what ails you."[1] They took advantage of naïve people who lacked good sense. Today, various laws protect consumers from being duped by outlandish claims. But there are always loopholes in these truth-in-advertising laws.

It's said that numbers don't lie, but people can manipulate numbers to deceive people. Remember the Enron scandal where executives and accounting firms profited by using some creative accounting, also known as "cooking the books?"[2] And how about Bernie Madoff's Ponzi scheme of investing that duped so many people out of billions of dollars?[3] It's easy to fool people when they want to believe what they want to hear.

Opinion polls are often used to verify certain beliefs or statements. The implication is that if a certain amount of people or a majority percentage hold an opinion, then this is the prevailing wisdom or truth. Regardless of how many people hold an opinion, it doesn't make it true or wise.

Neither truth nor wisdom is based on majority opinions.

insights

At the beginning of Ecclesiastes chapter 10, Solomon expresses several proverbial sayings. They may seem somewhat random but they continue a theme begun in the previous chapter. Keep in mind that the author did not divide the original writings into chapters and verses. We need to connect the thought of the first verse of chapter 10 to the last line of chapter nine, *"one sinner can destroy much that is good."* The picture of dead flies in a bottle of perfumed ointment is clear. Not only is it a disgusting image—it stinks! Here's how Solomon explains the foul odor of the flies in the ointment—

> *"A little foolishness outweighs wisdom and honor." (Ecclesiastes 10:1 GW).*

This tells us how destructive indiscretion is upon a person's integrity. More than a few powerful leaders have lost their influence because of their indiscretions. Character matters. The flaws in a person's character may often outweigh their accomplishments and wisdom. King Solomon is a prime example of this. As always, many of these proverbial sayings need to be understood from their ancient perspective. Keep this in mind throughout Ecclesiastes. Especially with what Solomon says in verse 2, as he compares wisdom and foolishness—

> *A wise man's heart is at his right hand, But a fool's heart at his left. (Ecclesiastes 10:2 NKJV)*

In ancient times, the "right hand" stood as a sign of authority, strength, and even favor. Solomon contrasts the heart of the wise with a foolish person's heart—"at his left." The next verse continues to explore the contrast between the wise and the foolish. The advice in verse 4 calls for discretion. It also provides some practical guidance relevant for today—

> *If a ruler becomes angry with you, don't resign your position. If you remain calm, you can make up for serious offenses. (Ecclesiastes 10:4 GW)*

It's easier to give in to failure than to overcome it.

Overcoming failure requires a commitment and willingness to accept responsibility for our failures and wrongs without reacting with defensiveness or self-justification. Repairing a relationship and improving our standing with those who are in authority or leadership roles in our lives is where discretion comes in along with discernment. A sense of precaution and practical wisdom apply to the remaining verses, especially the *"dull ax."* In fact, verse 10 has relevance for today aside from chopping wood.

existential reflections for everyday life

"Work smarter, not harder" is a popular saying nowadays. It can apply to a lot of work situations and even to relationships. *"Wisdom prepares the way for success"* is an older version of *work smarter, not harder*, as illustrated by sharpening a dull ax. How to *work smarter, not harder* in relation to working with others requires discernment and discretion.

The first thing to do is understand (discern) how to *"sharpen the edge"* of the proverbial ax. Second, we need to see how to apply whatever insight we have for sharpening the edge. This is where discretion comes in, especially in relating to others—whether they are colleagues, friends, or family members. While working with other people and working under various leaders, I came to realize the need to understand each person for who they are. I needed to learn what motivates them, what they value, and how best to communicate with them.[4]

When I worked under another leader in the same ministry, I realized he wanted to make the final decisions but wanted my input on various options. When working on a project, I'd give him two or three options and let him decide. These were options I saw as good and workable for me in my role of leadership. After my supervisor processed it all, he based his decision on one or more of the options I gave him. I also communicated more details and information than he required, which worked well for us for many years.

I also found overseeing staff and pastoring a church was like parenting. My wife and I raised four children and parented many foster children in the US and overseas. Both of us had strong points and not-so-strong points. We learned how to work together in a partnership as parents of children with many distinct personalities and in many situations. We learned to be flexible, and we realized who was best at handling certain personalities in various situations.

Here are some essential elements for gaining the useful wisdom of discernment and discretion.

- **Learn to listen well**—with attentiveness and respect
- **Be observant**—as the ancient adage goes, look before you leap
- **Don't react or overreact**—be patient and considerate
- **Process before making a commitment or plan**—think things through to a result and beyond the moment
- **Focus on one thing at a time**—multitasking is a foolish delusion[5]

Do you have any more ideas on how to be discerning and use discretion?

Practical wisdom will pave the way for success, whether in accomplishments or good relationships.

26 /
the vacuous and verbose nature of a fool

A wise person's words win favors, but a fool's lips are self-destructive. A fool starts out by talking foolishness and ends up saying crazy things that are dangerous. He never stops talking. (Ecclesiastes 10:12-14 GW)

[context– Ecclesiastes 10:11-20 GW]

the nature of words

I learned how words have meanings assigned to them during our family's preparation and training for cross-cultural mission work. As we learned new vocabulary words in the language we studied, the words seemed arbitrary and odd to us. We saw this played out repeatedly in our life overseas. In Cebuano, the local dialect where we lived in the Philippines, we use the word *pila* in counting or measuring by number. But the major dialect in Luzon is Tagalog, where *pila* means to line up in a queue or straight line. When a cashier at a bus terminal asked how many tickets were to be purchased, she said, *"Pila?"* Our pastor friends from Luzon lined up in a queue because they heard *"pila"* as, "line up!" If you knew Filipino culture, this would bring a chuckle since Filipinos rarely form lines the way westerners do.

American pastors and missionaries often use English words, even biblical words, that aren't understood by people who know English as a second or third language. Instead of explaining uncommon words in English in simpler words or terms, they assume and expect their listeners to understand what they say. This poses a problem for interpreters. Some words (even biblical ones) don't have an equivalent word or meaning in other languages. I've witnessed this many times. The interpreter either ignores what they say, makes something up, or asks for an explanation the speaker often can't give.

Words are symbolic. They convey ideas, feelings, thoughts, and even complex concepts. Words only have meaning because of how they're used or misused in a specific context. Words can be meaningful or meaningless—it depends a lot on who is saying them, along with their intent and motivation. Using words can be wise or foolish. Two obvious examples of how words can be wise or foolish are in social media and politics. This is especially true in what I'd call the age of misinformation. Several decades ago, someone coined the term Information Age.[1] It's safe to say we could describe the twenty-first century as the *Misinformation Age*.

insights

This segment of verses in the middle of Ecclesiastes chapter ten doesn't need a lot of explanation. Since a fool *"never stops talking,"* it's only wise to not say too much. One verse that needs some clarity is verse 11. I prefer the way it's written in the NKJV rather than in several other versions (including GW). It fits the context better than any attempt to be more literal with the translation.—

> *A serpent may bite when it is not charmed; The babbler is*
> *no different.*

Figurative language and proverbial sayings need to be understood within their original contexts—historical and cultural—and taken as the author intended. The rest of the verses are fairly easy to discern. The contrast between the words of the wise person and a fool is more about their integrity of character than just their words. Perhaps we see this contrast most clearly in verse 12—

> *A wise person's words win favors, but a fool's lips are self-destructive. (GW)*

Verse 15 drives the point home with the implication the fool doesn't even know what is obvious to everyone else. All the fool says and does is pointless. He has no grounding in what's true and all he says and does lack purpose. Here's a simple summary of these five verses—

- A wise person is gracious and purposeful with their words because they have integrity of character.
- A foolish person wounds and wearies himself and others with his words because the fool is vacuous (empty) and verbose (overly wordy) by nature.

existential reflections for everyday life

What we can learn from these few verses is simple, as is the application for our own lives. What could be difficult for some of us is to discern which person we are more like than the other. Perhaps each of us has played the role of a foolish person at certain times in life or even several days in a week—maybe more than we realize. I know this to be true for myself.

We all talk too much about what interests us most. We repeat what we've heard others say without verifying how true or reliable they are or if what they said is accurate. On social media, we see this a lot. I cringe when I know something that's said or repeated is neither accurate nor truthful. I cringe because I've said similar things, only to realize later how wrong I was. Although it's said in a different context, what Solomon said earlier in Ecclesiastes also seems appropriate as a practical application of these few verses in chapter ten—

> *Don't be in a hurry to talk. Don't be eager to speak in the presence of God. Since God is in heaven and you are*

> *on earth, limit the number of your words. (Ecclesiastes 5:2 GW)*

The apostle James echoes this thought—

> *Remember this, my dear brothers and sisters: Everyone should be quick to listen, slow to speak, and should not get angry easily. (James 1:19 GW)*

Later he says—

> *... the tongue is a small part of the body, but it can brag about doing important things. A large forest can be set on fire by a little flame.*
> *The tongue is that kind of flame. It is a world of evil among the parts of our bodies, and it completely contaminates our bodies. The tongue sets our lives on fire, and is itself set on fire from hell. (James 3:5-6 GW)*

Solomon puts a fine point on it when he says—

> *Sin is unavoidable when there is much talk, but whoever seals his lips is wise. (Proverbs 10:19 GW)*

It's hard to miss the point of all this. Just remember the adage—*God gave us two ears and one mouth for good reason.* If we can remember this, we'll be the wiser for it and so will others.

The wise person gains favor with people with their words, but the fool self-destructs with their words.

study questions for ecclesiastes chapter 10

For a more thorough study, read through Ecclesiastes Chapter 10 again to consider and answer the following questions—

1. How is foolishness likened to dead flies and contrasted with the wise?
2. How is a wise person's heart compared to a foolish one?
3. What are some ways foolishness is given importance that doesn't make sense?
4. How can wisdom help a person when things go wrong?
5. How do the examples given in verses 8-11 relate to what's said before them?
6. What else are we told about fools and foolish talk?
7. When have you said or done rash things you've regretted? What prompted these?
8. How do you handle situations where you're criticized, treated unfairly, or insulted?
9. Have you learned how to handle criticism and insults in wiser ways than before?
10. Do you have people in your life who are good examples of wise living?
11. Are you willing to learn from these people and their examples?

the improbable certainty and mystery of faith

Just as you don't know how the breath of life enters the limbs of a child within its mother's womb, you also don't understand how God, who made everything, works. (Ecclesiastes 11:5 GW) [context– Ecclesiastes 11:1-6 GW]

improbable certainty

I've been concerned for some time about parenting in our American culture. Although my wife and I came from typical but somewhat dysfunctional family settings, we set out to raise our family differently. We wanted our children to be healthy in an all-around sense. Thankfully, the Lord guided us along the way in this commitment. Though we read a bit of parenting advice, common sense was most helpful. When we started our family, parenting advice was minimal compared to what's available today. But more information is not always helpful. In fact, much of what's available seems counter to common sense and is way too subjective and relativistic.

"Helicopter parents" and "lawnmower parents" are two common forms of parenting today.[1] There's also a group of parents called "Tiger parents."[2] None of these types of parenting are healthy. That's not just my opinion—it's understood by teachers who deal with these parents and psychologists who look at it clinically. These overbearing and controlling parenting styles are an attempt to eliminate risks to their children.[3]

But there's no such thing as a risk-free life. Many people may think they want a risk-free life, but it's a delusion. Such certainty in life is not attainable. If—against all probability—you gained a risk-free life, it wouldn't be much of a life. The movie, The Truman Show,[4] depicts a choreographed risk-free reality-show life, portraying an idyllic life for Truman. But when Truman realizes he's living a scripted risk-free life, he tries to escape it.

Sure, we all would like to skip or avoid certain difficulties in our lives. But if everything in life was predictable and planned out, it would be boring and pointless. And yet, many people believe in fate, as if everything in life is predetermined. Fate is *not* faith. If anything, fate is a counterfeit faith. The essence of faith is trust—an implicit and personal trust in God (Hebrews 11:6). Fate is blind. Challenging or testing fate is like hope against hope. Some people imagine that abandoning themselves to whatever fate brings is an act of faith. It isn't. Fate is arbitrary. It's capricious. True, genuine faith is not blind but sees beyond circumstances and what appears predetermined or set. Faith is an assurance with hope in a living God.

When we invest our time, energy, and money in some venture, there is always an inherent risk. No one can predict the future accurately all the time. Some people can predict certain things will take place based on probabilities and various calculations. But most of us aren't able to do this.

The natural world is an illustration board designed by the hand of God. We can draw lessons from the cycles and seasons of the natural world. These lessons may apply to farming or business or our interaction with others. The natural world teaches us about the inherent risks in life. But as the saying goes—nothing ventured, nothing gained.

**Seeking a risk-free life is a feeble attempt to control life.
Such an attempt defies fate and scorns faith.**

insights

Chapter eleven begins with Solomon delivering several proverbial sayings before bringing his collection of existential reflections to a conclusion. At first glance, this may seem an odd and almost random group of thoughts. But there's a theme tying them together leading to the conclusion.

Throwing bread out on the water isn't some superstitious custom but a figurative expression. It could allude to the risks and rewards of shipping grain across the seas, which may be what Solomon has in mind. But this expression could also be an encouragement towards generosity. When we link verse 2 with the first verse, the second half of this poetic and proverbial couplet suggests there's a risk to being generous, but it's a wise risk.

Verse 2 reminds me of the commonly misunderstood parable of Jesus about an unjust yet shrewd steward. When his master intends to hold the steward accountable, the steward makes discount deals with those who are indebted to the master. His master commended the steward for creating options and building bridges of relationship with his discounted deals to the debtors (Luke 16:8-9). There's more to the story, but here's the point. The unjust steward set aside his greed in a way that benefited those who owed debts to his master. He looked beyond his own greedy desires as he realized his future need. Generosity can be more than a gesture of goodwill. It can also be a wise decision.

Verse 3 is a reminder of the cycles and seasons in the natural world that correspond to what we know as cause and effect—certain conditions and events bring about and precede other events or results. The natural result of rain-drenched clouds is the rain falling upon the land. The law of gravity results in a tree falling in a certain direction and staying there. Many events in life are obvious and predictable. As

Solomon declared before, there is a season and purpose for all things in life (Ecclesiastes 3:1-8).

In verse 4, we have the flip side of verse 1. The law of sowing and reaping is similar to cause and effect. A farmer who tries to determine the perfect time to sow a crop or reap a harvest without risk will end up doing neither. This illustration reminds us of a person who is fearful of taking risks and looks for the perfect time to act. It also speaks of a person who lacks conviction and commitment. A person who is risk-averse struggles with true faith. A person of faith accepts and understands the natural laws of cause and effect and of sowing and reaping. They also realize the many things beyond their grasp to understand or control.

We can take the last verse of this segment as an exhortation to live by faith along with a generous heart. Again, faith is an act of trust in God —not in ourselves, nor in fate, nor in nature.

> **Genuine faith requires a conviction and commitment to trust in God.**

existential reflections for everyday life

A sign of maturity is an awareness of certain realities in life. As a child grows and matures, they learn to accept and take on age-appropriate responsibilities. Education provides a child with the opportunity to learn about the world beyond their family and home. Learning and developing a sense of personal responsibility in life is an important part of the progression of maturity.

Raising children can be a challenge. I take that back—it *is* a challenge. A challenge that seems to increase exponentially with their age. This is especially true with strong-willed children. When children are young, they're more dependent on their parents, and parents can exert more control. But this changes as children age. They assert their free will in different ways, striving for independence. Each of our four children came to faith at a young age. Because I was a pastor, they were always involved with what we did in ministry. As they became teenagers, they gained more freedom. But with those freedoms, their responsibilities increased. They each learned to live by their own faith as they matured in their lives. This needed to happen. None of us can live by the faith of our parents or mentors. This is an important mark of spiritual maturity.

Another indicator of true maturity is to recognize various limitations in life—a person's own limitations and the existence of what is beyond our control in the world. We can't control the weather. Neither can we defy gravity. We can suspend the effect of gravity, but only temporarily and weather forecasts are reliably unreliable. We can't predict the future with accuracy and consistency. Even with all our scientific discoveries and learning, there are many things about life itself we still can't explain with certainty.

We also don't understand God—the Creator of life. This is one reason faith and fate may seem similar. But they're not. Faith and fate are vastly different. Fate is impersonal. Fate is arbitrary and often seen as unfair. It is the effect of some predetermined cause. When a person says they've accepted their fate in life, they resign themselves to a capricious and unknown destiny—like gambling based on betting odds.

Faith is personal. Genuine faith is based on our trust in God, who is the Creator and Sustainer of life and who gives purpose to our life. A person of faith is free to take risks because they trust in God rather than an unknown outcome. Their faith enables them to see beyond immediate circumstances and what may seem pointless and unfair.

When you or I live by faith, we can be generous because we trust in God's goodness and faithfulness. We can take reasonable risks based on experience and wisdom gained through trusting in God. As said many times by many people, "I don't know what the future holds, but I know who holds the future."

What about you? Are you still seeking a risk-free life?

Have you abandoned yourself to fate?

Or...

Have you learned to trust in God by faith?

28 /
the seductive appeal
of youth and
nostalgia

Even though people may live for many years, they should enjoy every one of them. But they should also remember there will be many dark days...

Get rid of what troubles you or wears down your body, because childhood and youth are pointless. (Ecclesiastes 11:8, 10 GW)

[context– Ecclesiastes 11:7-10 GW]

fleeting youth

I love baseball. I became a lifelong Los Angeles Dodgers fan when they moved from Brooklyn to LA. After the lights were out, I'd listen to games on my little transistor radio, hearing Vin Scully masterfully describe the game being broadcast.[1] He could make it come alive in ways few other announcers could. I realize this reveals my age bracket. Who even uses transistor radios nowadays? Vin Scully recently passed away and our national pastime is struggling to stay relevant. Still, I'll watch a baseball game on TV in the background as I do other things, read, or just relax.

I wanted to be a good baseball player when I was young, but I wasn't a naturally gifted athlete. I lacked confidence in myself. But in my daydreams, while listening to Vin Scully's technicolor narration of the game, I imagined myself making great plays or game-winning hits. In my thirties, I started playing slow-pitch softball. I still wasn't a talented athlete, but I could hold my own on the field with hustle and determination. Now, years later, I still daydream of making great plays and hits in my imagination. But it's a far cry from reality!

Try as we may, none of us can hang on to our youth. Our youth is a fleeting phase of life. It doesn't seem to last much longer than a firework display on the 4th of July. And yet, we revisit memories of this short-lived phase of life as we grow older. Even in our later years, it's common to think of ourselves in our younger persona. In our mind's eye, we see ourselves doing what our bodies will no longer tolerate.

Companies market thousands and thousands of products to slow down the aging process or attempt to rewind the biological clock. Lotions and cosmetics guarantee to eliminate wrinkles. Certain diet and exercise regimens claim amazing restorative power. And if all else fails, well, there are cosmetic surgery options. But none of these efforts can stop the aging process as we march toward our last breath. Our internal clocks tick away. It's only interrupted by catastrophic illness or tragic and premature death.

This is the reality of *life under the sun*. And yet, life is precious—every moment—even in the more difficult and dark periods of life. Those darker, more difficult times underscore the immeasurable value of life —just as the light of the stars pierces through the vastness of the night sky. God wants us to keep in mind how precious life is, as glimmers of light amid dark times.

Why are we so infatuated with youth? We realize its precious value as we grow older. We see this with how enraptured elderly people are with babies and young children. Now that we have grandchildren, I look back on the early days of raising our children. Of course, I see certain traits and likenesses of our four grown children in their children. This stirs memories and stories to tell at family gatherings. I remember the anticipation of each birth. What will they look like? Who will they resemble most? And we enjoyed watching their little personalities grow in the early stages of development. Well, most of the time we enjoyed it.

One day, I mentioned my fond memories of our children when they were young, and my wife reminded me how hard it was for her. It was easier for me than for her. I was out of the house busy with my ministry work while she cared for the children. Being a mom of four energetic kids and a wife of a full-time pastor was far more stressful for my wife than I realized then. I appreciate it more now. Still, I look back on those days with fondness. I sometimes wish we could go back to enjoy that time once again somehow. *Sigh*. But that's just selective memory on my part, not unlike my baseball daydreams.

We need to guard against the seduction of nostalgia and envying those who are younger. When we allow ourselves to be snared with envy or lost in nostalgia, we miss the significance of each present and passing moment in our life.

Envy and nostalgia can rob us of the value and worth of everyday life when we ignore the present.

insights

These few verses at the end of chapter eleven start with a pleasant thought but finish with a return to Solomon's cynical view of *life under the sun*. But by digging deeper, we can catch his main point.

Studies have verified the beneficial effect of sunlight.[2] It's the most readily available and natural source of vitamin D, which is an important element of a healthy immune system. Sunlight is also a major factor for psychological health, both emotional and mental. Geographic areas that lack sunlight exposure often see an increase in alcoholism/addiction, depression, and even an increase in suicide attempts attributed to SAD (seasonal affective disorder). Here's the heart of what Solomon is saying—

> *Light is sweet, and it is good for one's eyes to see the sun.*
> *Even though people may live for many years, they*
> *should enjoy every one of them. (Ecclesiastes 11:7-*
> *8 GW)*

Will dark days come? Yes. Will *life under the sun* seem pointless some-times? Yes. Enjoying life in simple ways and while the sun shines in our life—when life is pleasant—helps us overcome times of darkness. It provides us with a healthy perspective, like a bridge over the dark times of life.

Solomon then turns his exhortation from those who are older to the young. But his encouragement to the young includes a warning—one Solomon will expand on further in the final chapter of Ecclesiastes. Solomon encourages young people to enjoy their youth while it lasts. Curiosity and an idealistic outlook on life typically characterize our youth. Even for those with difficult, even dangerous childhoods, hope for better days seems embedded in their hearts and dreams.

But there's a caveat to Solomon's encouragement to *"follow wherever your heart leads you"* in verse 9. A time will come when God will hold all people to account for their lives, as said in the last verse of Ecclesi-astes (Ecclesiastes 12:14). Solomon's concluding thought in this chapter is to jettison whatever burdens us, including the anxiety and stress that take a toll on us physically as well as mentally. Remember, childhood and youth don't last long and *life under the sun* is also brief compared to eternity.

existential reflections for everyday life

There's a place for nostalgia in our lives. We could say the only place for nostalgia is in the past, but that would be a state of denial. We all have memories. Some are treasures we hold close to our hearts, while others remind us of difficult or dark times. Whenever I preside at a funeral or memorial service, I remind those gathered of the value of memories. They are treasures we hold in our hearts and minds. And as we age, we gather more memories, both recent and past. All of us are a composite of our memories. They are pieces of experience that make up the mosaic of our lives.

Nostalgia is a selective time of remembrance. We connect the word to homesickness—a longing for and wistful remembrance of family and home. We all remember our childhood and youth with selective memory. This is what high school reunions thrive on and why our nostalgia typically focuses on "the good old days." We need to guard against dwelling on nostalgic memories carrying us on a dreamlike sentimental journey. It's not reality. It's a state of denial.

But nostalgia can have a good purpose. Those of us who are grandparents understand how quickly time passes, especially childhood and youth. I often encourage young parents to enjoy their children while they're young, especially while they are babies. Sure, there's lots of lost sleep, but this precious time passes so quickly.

Yes, raising children has its challenges, and family life can be overwhelming. Many of us struggled to make ends meet while trying to keep up with the ever-changing dynamics of home life and the demands and troubles of *life under the sun*. This is where the American way of life may put us at a disadvantage with other cultures. We put a high value on independence and single-family homes, while many other cultures put a high value on community life with multi-generational home settings. Each has its challenges and drawbacks.

In our youth, we think we're indestructible, even immortal. But it's a delusion. As we age, selective fantasies of our younger days can seduce us into dreamy nostalgia. But idolizing youth and our younger years doesn't make us young again.

Each generation can be a blessing to other generations if we choose to be so.

Children learn from their parents and grandparents, both the good and the bad. We may want young people to respect those who are older. But those of us who are older need to value and respect younger generations. If we want respect, we need to show it to others, even those younger than ourselves. We can all learn from one another, but this requires respect for one another.

Just as today's technology is native to younger people, a valuable aspect of older generations is a historical perspective. Young generations would be wise to learn from and respect those older than themselves. Experience is valuable, especially when that experience came at a cost, as it often does. Older generations have valuable lessons and remembrances to pass on to younger generations.

Youth is fleeting, and nostalgia has some value. But remember—"*Light is sweet and pleasant.*" It's more powerful than darkness. *Life under the sun* won't last long, so enjoy it while you can and remember the light in times of darkness.

Life is precious—every moment, every day, and every year.

study questions for ecclesiastes chapter 11

For a more thorough study, read through Ecclesiastes Chapter 11 again to consider and answer the following questions—

1. What are we encouraged to do in verses 1-2 and why?
2. What can we count on and what can't we be sure of?
3. What do we not know, and what advice follows this reality?
4. What realities are certain, and how should this affect how we live our lives?
5. What advice and caution are given to young people?
6. How does this caution relate to the advice given at first?
7. How often do you allow what you can't control in life to control you?
8. How has doing good returned to you in some way?
9. When have you not taken a risk and wished you did? When have you been glad you took a risk?
10. What have you learned from the foolish things you've done earlier in life? How have these experiences benefited you?

29 /

remember your creator before your life slips into eternity

Remember your Creator when you are young, before the days of trouble come and the years catch up with you. They will make you say, "I have found no pleasure in them." (Ecclesiastes 12:1 GW)

[context– Ecclesiastes 12:1-5 GW]

the passing of time

Unexpected things can happen at unexpected times and in unexpected ways. As a pastor, I presided over too many funerals that seemed premature and far too early. These were tough services to officiate as their pastor, and each of their stories grieved me.

I had a good friend who left a beautiful young wife and two young children after a prolonged battle with cancer. The death of a young spouse is hard, like another young man who died a tragic death on his motorcycle when someone turned in front of him. He left behind a young wife and child, and I was at a loss for how to comfort her. But the death of a child is even tougher to deal with. This hit home when a five-year-old boy's heart stopped because a baseball hit him in the chest. It was a freak accident. He was in my five-year-old son's Sunday school class and his parents were new believers in our church. The grief is so palpable that it still grabs me four decades later.

When death pushes itself into our lives, it's a reminder of how temporary life is. If we're willing to reflect on our own lives, we can realize how our focus on life, death, and the time in between is so subjective. Time is constant. There are sixty seconds in a minute, sixty minutes in an hour, twenty-four hours in a day, and so on with weeks, months, and years, as the earth makes its journey around the sun marked by the changing seasons. But time can also be arbitrary and relative.

Time seems to pass at different speeds in different phases of life. Newborns depend on their parents, especially their mothers, and spend most of their time all bundled up and asleep. Within weeks, they are balancing on their tummies and taking everything in, and before you know it, they crawl, then walk. From birth to preschool age (four and five years old), the continuing changes in a child's development are remarkable. As they develop, children strive for independence —from learning the word "no" to wanting to do everything themselves.

Those early years seem to fly by until school starts. Then time seems to slow down and even go too slowly from the perspective of the child. They can't wait to turn six and look forward to the next birthday and the next one, as each year passes. Each milestone birthday brings greater status and more freedoms or privileges.

Along the way, parents may realize how quickly their children are growing up. Some may regret not spending more time with them when they were younger. And too soon, it may seem, children move forward with more independence from mom and dad into adulthood, college, and careers. For parents, time may seem to slow a bit to a more measured pace during the school years. But once our children grow up, they pursue their own lives and raise their own families. The years seem to pass faster and faster.

Toddlers and preschoolers don't relate to time the way adults do. I often think these young children have a much better sense of eternity than adults because everything is now for them. I'm also realizing time is much more relative for the elderly, especially as their death becomes imminent. Watching the end-of-life stage for three parents for two decades, I'm more aware of this. Time seems to slow down and memories of younger times are more vivid. In the end, at the edge of eternity, their perception of time is like that of toddlers. We are bound by the continuum of time in this *life under the sun*, but eternity lies beyond.

insights

The poetic exhortation, *"Remember your Creator when you are young,"* links back to chapter eleven. The first seven verses of chapter twelve extend the thoughts expressed in the last two verses of chapter eleven. I've chosen to focus on the first five verses of chapter twelve here to show how the opening thoughts of Ecclesiastes come full circle. Solomon begins with his cynical view of *life under the sun*, adding some existential questions and thoughts echoed by many others before and after Solomon's time.

It's significant that Solomon uses the phrase—*Remember your Creator.* By describing God as the Creator, Solomon acknowledges that *life under the sun* has a purpose and that God is personal, though this seems contradictory to his previous thoughts about life being pointless. In the original text, the opening phrase—Remember your Creator—is only found in verse one, but implied for each stanza of the poetic expressions in the first six verses. This is why and how it's worded this way in GOD'S WORD Translation (GW).[1]

Each verse is a poetic stanza, with extended thoughts describing the latter days of *life under the sun*. These first six verses directly contrast the encouragement and warning given to young people in verse 9 of the previous chapter. The exhortation of the first five verses encourages young people to remember God is their Creator and there will come a time when their strength will fade and *life under the sun* will end. Then they will face their Creator to account for their lives.

Consider these descriptive thoughts contrasted with young people's sense of freedom and invincibility. *"Remember your Creator when you are young, before…"*

- … *the days of trouble come… years catch up… no pleasure in them.*
- … *the sun, light, moon, stars turn dark… clouds… with rain.*
- … *those who guard… tremble… strong men… stooped… women at the mill stop grinding… [people] see a dim light.*
- … *afraid of heights… dangers… almond tree blossoms… grasshopper drags… caper bush… no fruit. (Ecclesiastes 12:1-5 GW)*

A grasshopper's life cycle is about one year and the almond tree blossoms in early February—wintertime. Each of these verses describes the progression and characteristics of old age and the end of life. Desire and pleasure don't have the same pull as before. People you've grown up with are also aging and dying. Physical capacities—including hearing, sight, and strength—weaken and wane. Fears magnify and the mind drifts from reality as the end of life draws near.

In the end, each life fades into eternity while others mourn.

existential reflections for everyday life

My wife and I have witnessed this end-of-life stage while caring for our parents. It's hard to watch and difficult to navigate. It also makes us mindful of our aging. When talking with my aunt who turned one hundred-one a year ago, she told us how lonely she was since the death of her friends and family members whom she's survived. She especially misses her sister (my mom) who passed away just before Covid-19 hit. The isolation of lockdowns magnified her sense of loneliness.

Why did Solomon exhort young people to remember their Creator while they were young? Studies show young people who come to faith at an early age are more likely to continue in their faith as they age.[2] Conversely, as people age without faith in God, it is often harder for them to believe in God. Why? This is the primary purpose of the book of Ecclesiastes. Solomon didn't write this book to encourage or promote cynicism. His agenda wasn't to persuade people toward a nihilistic view of life—it was the exact opposite.

Reading through this poetic description of the end-of-life stage ought to encourage us to reflect on the value and purpose of our lives now. Regardless of our current age, this is a reminder that each of us will eventually enter eternity while living *under the sun* continues for others.

Again, time is a relative concept, especially as we live in an era with longer life expectancies. What we considered old age in the past is now looked upon as "the golden years." Those who qualify for senior discounts are more active and freer to enjoy life than in previous generations. True, this is a generalization and doesn't apply to everyone, but it is the trend.

The questions you should consider now rather than later are—

Where do things stand between you and your Creator?

Do you believe in God as the Creator of all life?

Do you realize each of us will give an account of our life after death?

It's better to consider these questions before life slips away, and we enter eternity, because—

Time is short. Life is precious. Eternity is forever.
And God, our Creator, is real and personal.

the hard truths of life, death, grief, and eternity

Remember your Creator before the silver cord is snapped, the golden bowl is broken, the pitcher is smashed near the spring, and the water wheel is broken at the cistern.

Then the dust *of mortals* goes back to the ground as it was before, and the breath of life goes back to God who gave it. "Absolutely pointless!" says the spokesman. "Everything is pointless!" (Ecclesiastes 12:6-8 GW)

[context– Ecclesiastes 12:1-8 GW]

grief and grieving

My role as a pastor, as it is for any pastor, required me to deal with grief more often than I chose and with many people over the years. Honestly, I wasn't ready to handle this responsibility at first. So, I read about grief to understand it as best I could. I learn to listen and say little, and just be present with those who mourned. I saw people grieve in different ways and in their own time.

Grief is something my wife and I dealt with as overseas missionaries. Children who were under our care and some of our staff died while we were on the mission field. And we experienced the loss of siblings, parents, and grandparents in our lifetime. We were overseas when Susan lost her dad to Alzheimer's. Her family notified me of this at the airport while on my way back to the Philippines. In those days, we both couldn't be gone from our ministry at the same time. I went back to the States for some ministry business while Susan was back in the Philippines. We crossed in the air, going in opposite directions.

The reality of grief is unavoidable and shows up, and in ways, we don't expect. Perhaps we expect the death of a loved one in cases of a long-term illness, but grief still imposes itself on us in unexpected ways and times.

But grief isn't just about death. Grief is a response to a loss. Grief can be physical and psychological,[1] but it's always real. In a general sense, Americans often deny grief and stuff it or push through it as swiftly as possible—at least on an individual level. We don't know what to do with grief.[2] I think we do anger better than sadness. There are exceptions, of course. When a natural disaster impacts whole towns or a tragic event like the terrorism of the 9/11 tragedy impacts the nation, we grieve together.

But even when we experience grief as an entire community or nation, we are quick to work at recovering from the disaster or tragedy. Often, outside help comes to assist with the recovery. This is a wonderful trait. We Americans do recovery work better than grief work. Too often, we set aside the actual work of grief to do the work of recovery. And yet, as said earlier, grief is unavoidable. If we don't go through a healthy grieving process, it will cost us later in life.

insights

These few verses in chapter twelve are a poetic description of the end of *life under the sun*. The four metaphorical phrases in verse 6 are euphemisms—ways to describe death more pleasantly. They lead to the finality of Solomon's statement in verse 7. We use many euphemisms for death. People have done this since ancient days. Instead of saying, "they're dead," we use expressions like—"he's passed away... gone to meet his Maker... asleep in Christ... or entered eternity." Of course, there are some not-so-nice euphemistic expressions for death like, "kicked the bucket... pushing up daisies... or six-feet-under." Death is the final stage of *life under the sun.*

For those of us who trust in God, death is not the final stage of life itself. Solomon implied this in verse 7 and verse 9 of chapter eleven. Earlier in Ecclesiastes, he reminds us why we have hope beyond physical death and raises questions about *life under the sun* and life after death.

> *He has made everything beautiful in its time. Also He has put eternity in their hearts, except that no one can find out the work that God does from beginning to end. (Ecclesiastes 3:11 NKJV)*

There are two primary thoughts Solomon would have us consider in verse 7 of chapter twelve—

- *life under the sun* has a beginning and an end
- *life under the sun* is temporary when contrasted to eternity

When God created humanity, He made our physical bodies from the basic elements of the earth (dust) and breathed life into us (spirit) so we became living beings (Genesis 2:7). The burial of the body and return of the spirit to God is the cycle of *life under the sun,* as Solomon put it earlier—

> *To everything there is a season, A time for every purpose under heaven: (Ecclesiastes 3:1 NKJV)*

And yet, compared to eternity, *life under the sun* is short. It's easy to have a cynical view of this as *pointless, futile,* or *vanity.* But we need to go back to the original word in Hebrew that is translated as pointless —it's *hevel.* In its literal sense, it means wind, breath, or vapor. But its figurative sense gives us the idea of lacking substance or concrete existence, giving the idea of everything being pointless, futile, or in vain—that is, temporary or unsubstantial.

Life under the sun is pointless unless we acknowledge God as our Creator who gives purpose to our lives and provides us with hope beyond life on earth because we trust in Him.

existential reflections for everyday life

Grief is an emotional response to a loss or major change in our life. When we lose someone we love, it's a major change in our life. And major life changes bring certain losses, as we all experienced with the Covid-19 pandemic. Everyone grieves in different ways, and the grieving process has different stages. There is much written and said about what a healthy grieving process is. But I've found this to be very personal for each of us.

Not long ago, I spoke with a woman who was grieving the loss of her husband, along with the many facets of their relationship. I encouraged her that no one fully knows her loss, though others may have similar experiences. She and her husband shared a relationship unique to them. As it says in Proverbs—

> *The heart knows its own bitterness, and no stranger can*
> *share its joy. (Proverbs 14:10 GW)*

I know my grieving process varies. Before my family and I moved to the Philippines, our church held a special service for us. We started the church and poured twelve years of our life into this ministry, and we held many close relationships with other families in the church. During a certain song, I burst out in a torrent of tears and grief. It took everyone by surprise, including me. When that expression of grief was over, I felt relieved and ready to move on.

My wife and I cared for both of my parents in their last years and I'm glad we did. But my grieving process for both of them differed from my emotional outburst before moving overseas. It was also different from my sister's experience with our parents' deaths. As I processed why this might be, I realized how I'd been grieving the loss of each of my parents before they died. I seemed to grieve in bits, little by little, as I saw their decline toward death.

When reading Solomon's description of death and dying in the first seven verses of chapter twelve, it resonates with me. Even the process of death and dying has a season and purpose to it when we take a step back to observe it as a whole.

When we are young, we need to *remember our Creator*. Life is a lot shorter than it seems when we're young and when we feel invincible and almost immortal. As we age, we need to remember our Creator before we get to the last stages of death and while in that end-of-life stage.

Each *life under the sun* has meaning and purpose.

Each life is a season within all the seasons of *life under the sun* among other generations.

One more thought about all this. Not only do we need to remember our Creator, but we also need to remind others about our Creator. This is of important significance in our lives *under the sun* for those of us who have a personal relationship with our Creator.

Our purpose as children of the Creator of all life is to be a living testimony of our Creator.

study questions for ecclesiastes chapter 12

For a more thorough study, read through Ecclesiastes Chapter 12 again to consider and answer the following questions—

1. What are we encouraged to remember while we are young and why?
2. How is the progression toward old age described?
3. Which of these descriptive phrases stands out to you?
4. What is the final reason given for remembering our Creator?
5. What is said about wise words and teaching?
6. What warning is given about sayings and writings?
7. What is the last advice given and what final thought underscores why this is important?
8. Are you content or concerned about the purpose of your life?
9. Can you see what tends to clutter up your life?
10. Are you able to find ways to simplify your life?
11. Do you spend time seeking wisdom from God?
12. Are there wise and godly people in your life?
13. Do you make time each day to connect with God?
14. Do you make room for Him in your life each day?

epilogue

Living Each Day with the End of Life in Mind

After having heard it all, this is the conclusion: Fear God, and keep his commands, because this applies to everyone. God will certainly judge everything that is done. This includes every secret thing, whether it is good or bad. (Ecclesiastes 12:13-14 GW)

[context– Ecclesiastes 12:9-14 GW]

---

what comes after death?

What do you think comes after death? Does it all just fade to black? Do we all go to heaven? Or do we get absorbed into the universe into a state of nothingness? Whatever you believe takes place after physical death will impact how you live your life—either directly or indirectly. If you give little thought to what lies beyond death, your daily life will reflect this lack of consideration. If you believe physical death is the end of any existence, then you may not care how you or anyone else lives their life. After all, why would it matter if there's no afterlife and things just fade to black? Many people hold this view, as reflected in their philosophical beliefs.

From a faith-based point of view, what we believe about life, death, and the afterlife *does* matter. It also ought to have a direct impact on how we live now. But does it? The Western mindset puts great emphasis on setting goals. Once we set a goal, we make a plan to achieve the goal, often with a schedule of smaller goals leading to the completion of the principal goal.

Too often, people apply this same goal-setting mindset to living the Christian life with their goal of going to heaven. It's seen as a practical way of living the Christian life, one that is considered good and meaningful. But this practical approach to the Christian life doesn't require a belief in God—the God of the Scriptures. A general term for this is Christian atheism.[1] It is a form of Christianity that rejects the theistic claims of Christianity.[2] Although there are similarities, don't confuse this with the book, *The Christian Atheist,* by Craig Groeschel, who says a Christian atheist is someone who believes in God, but who lives as though He doesn't exist.

When a person strives to live a *Christian life* but doesn't believe God exists or lives in a way that reflects a lack of belief in God, the life they lead is a moralistic version of Christianity.[3] It's an attempt to be Christ-like without genuine faith in God. Sadly, many people who profess to be Christians live this way. They lack genuine faith as defined in the Scriptures (Proverbs 3:5-6; Hebrews 11:1, 6).

Eternal life is not the goal of the Christian life. We can't gain it by living a good life. Eternal life is the gift and promise of God to those who trust in Him (see John 3:16, 36; 5:24; 17:3). If there were a goal for the Christian life, it would simply be this—to trust God in all things, at all times.

the point of it all

The last two verses of Ecclesiastes reveal the point of all of Solomon's existential reflections and seem to verify him as "the Preacher" or "Spokesman." Solomon collected and wrote many sayings in the book of Proverbs. I believe Ecclesiastes and Proverbs connect in the same sense as we see in verse 11—

> *Words from wise people are like spurs. Their collected*
> *sayings are like nails that have been driven in firmly.*
> *They come from one shepherd. (Ecclesiastes*
> *12:11 GW)*

Ecclesiastes acts like "spurs" to prompt introspection and reflection on the purpose and value of life. The wisdom in the book of Proverbs is practical wisdom to help people live their lives with the end of life in mind. Reading and processing the wisdom of Proverbs can be a valuable guide to help a person live a purposeful life—"*... like nails that have been driven in firmly.*"

These words of truth from "one shepherd"—possibly an allusion to the Lord as the ultimate author—provide a firm foundation for life. Solomon encourages us to keep things simple as a segue into his final thoughts on *life under the sun*. He returns to something he said at the beginning—

> *Be warned, my children, against anything more than*
> *these. People never stop writing books. Too much*
> *studying will wear out your body. (Ecclesiastes*
> *12:12 GW)*

Solomon seems to point us to the basic and practical wisdom in the Book of Proverbs. The conclusion is Solomon's wise exhortation in answer to all the questions about *life under the sun*—

> *Fear God, and keep his commands, because this applies to*
> *everyone. (Ecclesiastes 12:13 GW)*

During Solomon's time, the Law of the Covenant was the foundation for the relationship between God and His people. God intended the Covenant Law to guide His people to live a life reflecting their trust in and worship of the One, True, Living God. Israel, the nation, was a descendant of Abraham—a man of great faith and a friend of God (James 2:23). God called His people to be a living testimony of His existence.

The fear of God is the beginning of knowledge and wisdom, as Solomon points out at the beginning of Proverbs and throughout this collection of practical wisdom (Proverbs 1:7; 9:10). The fear of God is a biblical truth often ignored and misunderstood. It is not an anxious, paralyzing fear of terror. To fear God (in a biblical sense) means we have an awe and respect that motivates us to honor and worship God for who He is. The fear of the Lord is grounded in a personal relationship of trust. Solomon's final exhortation is a reminder of the final examination of our lives after death. It is a simple yet powerful reason to fear God and keep His commands.

existential questions we need to answer

What happens as we take our final breath and pass from life to death? As said earlier, whatever we believe takes place after physical death directly or indirectly impacts our life. Ignoring this question isn't wise. Putting off the inevitable doesn't resolve this question or make it go away. Dismissing it as nonsense won't enable anyone to avoid this ultimate reality. Subjects like the fear of God, commands, and eternal judgment aren't popular topics of discussion. They make us feel uncomfortable, or worse, they're of no interest to many people. Why is this? I'm sure there are many ways to answer this, but here's the simple reason—it requires us to consider our lives in the light of God's truth.

Some may ask—Why should we fear God if He is a God of love? Doesn't the Bible say, *"perfect love casts out fear"* (1 John 4:18)? Yes, but that verse speaks of a fear of torment, not a fear of respect for God. What about all those commandments? Jesus summed up the entire Law in two statements, as He pointed out to an expert in the Covenant Law. First, love and honor God with all your trust in Him. Second, love and respect others (Mark 12:28-34). So keep it simple, just as Jesus explained to the law expert. When those are our priorities, the rest will take care of itself, even as Jesus said in the Sermon on the Mount—

> *But seek first his kingdom and his righteousness, and all these things will be given to you as well. Therefore do*

not worry about tomorrow, for tomorrow will worry
about itself. Each day has enough trouble of its own.
(Matthew 6:33-34 NIV)

A concern about judgment should be a non-issue when it comes to a final assessment and judgment of our lives. After all, people make judgments and assess the lives and actions of others while they're alive. And this was true long before social media platforms. We are often our harshest critics. We judge ourselves throughout the day with self-talk no one else hears. And though Jesus cautions us *not* to judge others, we do so anyway.

Do you believe in a living, personal God? If so, trust in Him implicitly. God will answer these existential questions in a way that you can understand the answers. If you don't believe and trust in God, then you'll be wrestling with these existential questions throughout your *life under the sun*, and you'll continue to wonder about the value and purpose of your life.

Our biggest problem with questions about life, death, and the afterlife is their connection to our relationship with God or lack of one. All our questions about *life under the sun*, death, and what happens after physical death depend on where things stand between us and God.

The key to fearing God is to trust in God. God will honor and bless those who trust in Him.

notes

preface

1. Contributors to Wikimedia projects. "Wisdom Literature." *Simple English Wikipedia, the Free Encyclopedia*, 13 Jan. 2020, simple.wikipedia.org/wiki/Wisdom_literature.

    See also, Fee, Gordon, and Douglas Stuart. *How to Read the Bible for All Its Worth: Fourth Edition*. 4th ed., e-book, Zondervan Academic, 2014. (pages 238-240, 254)

2. ---. "Living Word Study Guide and Journal." *Word-Strong with Trip Kimball*, Word-Strong, 13 Aug. 2007, www.word-strong.com/shop/bible-study-set-cy983.

3. Enduring Word, and David Guzik. "Enduring Word - Free Bible Commentary from Pastor David Guzik." *Enduring Word*, enduringword.com. Accessed 1 Jan. 2020.

prologue

1. Kranz, Jeffrey. "TaNaKh: The 24 Books of the Hebrew Bible [Whiteboard Bible Study]." *OverviewBible*, 1 Sept. 2018, overviewbible.com/tanakh.

2. "Existentialism." *Wikiwand*, www.wikiwand.com/en/Existentialism. Accessed 19 Jan. 2021.

3. "Existence." *The Merriam-Webster.com Dictionary*, 17 Nov. 2022, www.merriam-webster.com/dictionary/existence.

4. "Wikiwand- Søren Kierkegaard." *Wikiwand*, www.wikiwand.com/en/S%C3%B8ren_Kierkegaard.

1. is there really anything new under the sun?

1. Contributors to Wikimedia projects. "Wisdom Literature." *Simple English Wikipedia, the Free Encyclopedia*, 13 Jan. 2020, simple.wikipedia.org/wiki/Wisdom_literature.

2. Messerly, John. "Summary of Existentialism." *Reason and Meaning*, 3 Nov. 2019, reasonandmeaning.com/2017/12/11/the-basic-ideas-of-existentialism/#.

2. if knowledge is power, can ignorance be bliss?

1. "Scientia Potentia Est." *Wikiwand*, www.wikiwand.com/en/Scientia_potentia_est. Accessed 11 Aug. 2021.

2. "Francis Bacon." *Wikiwand*, Wikipedia, www.wikiwand.com/en/Francis_Bacon. Accessed 11 Aug. 2021.

3. Tréguer, Pascal. "'Ignorance Is Bliss': Meaning and Origin." *Word Histories*, 1 Dec. 2020, wordhistories.net/2020/12/01/ignorance-bliss.

4. Kimball, Trip. "Christianity Is Not About Moral Goodness - Publishous." *Medium*, 26 Mar. 2021, medium.com/publishous/christianity-is-not-about-moral-goodness-bc2e1b0d09bc.

3. the problem with me, myself, and the pursuit of pleasure

1. ---. "Most of the Rest of the World—MOTROW —." *Word-Strong with Trip Kimball*, 16 Jan. 2018, www.word-strong.com/thinking-out-loud/most-of-the-rest-of-the-world-motrow-c3xk4.

2. "Me Generation." *Wikiwand*, www.wikiwand.com/en/Me_generation. Accessed 22 Sept. 2021.

3. Lewis, C. *Mere Christianity Combining the Case For Christianity, Christian Behaviour, Beyond Personality*. Macmillan, 1965. https://amzn.to/3kf1KDI

4. Aitken, Jonathan. "John Newton (Foreword by Philip Yancey): From Disgrace to Amazing Grace." *Amazon.Cm*, Crossway, 7 June 2007, amzn.to/3fvB9in.

5. Newton, John. *Out of the Depths*. USA, Kregel Publications, 2003.

6. Severance, Ph.D., Diane. "John Newton - the Story of Discovering Amazing Grace." *Christianity.Com*, 28 Apr. 2010, www.christianity.com/church/church-history/timeline/1701-1800/john-newton-discovered-amazing-grace-11630253.html.

4. our life's legacy ought to be a gift from god to others

1. Kimball, Trip. "Out of the Ashes - Publishous." *Medium*, Publishous, 10 Aug. 2021, medium.com/publishous/out-of-the-ashes-5b89ff1e8cef.

5. the cycles and seasons of life under the sun

1. ---. "The Cycles and Seasons of Life Under the Sun —." *Word-Strong With Trip Kimball*, 18 Aug. 2021, www.word-strong.com/home/the-cycles-and-seasons-of-life-under-the-sun-hc8t8.

2. ---. "Out of the Ashes - Publishous." *Medium*, 10 Aug. 2021, medium.com/publishous/out-of-the-ashes-5b89ff1e8cef.

6. god puts eternity in our hearts and makes all things beautiful

1. "Redemptive Analogies - A Key To The Heart- by Don Richardson." *https://www.missionresources.com/*,

3 Oct. 2013, www.missionresources.com/redemptiveanalogies.

2. Richardson, Don. *Eternity in Their Hearts by Don Richardson (8-MHttps://Www. Missionresources.Com/* Publishers; 3rd edition (8 Mar. 2006), 2021. https://amzn. to/34Xt0Bz

3. "MOW – Marian Anderson On Stage." *YouTube*, uploaded by https://www.y-outube.com/channel/UCMTBr2tAvnSNZd8i2X84pJw, 12 Aug. 2013, www. youtube.com/watch?v=2HfNovwcaX8.

4. "He's Got the Whole World in His Hands." *Wikiwand*, www.wikiwand.com/en/ He%27s_Got_the_Whole_World_in_His_Hands. Accessed 22 Sept. 2021.

5. undefined [RARE FACTS]. "I Have a Dream Speech by Mwww.wikiwand.com/ en/He%27s_Got_the_Whole_World_in_His_Hands, www.youtube.com/watch?v= vP4iY1TtS3s.

6. Lewis, C. *Mere Christianity (C. S. Lewis Signature Classic)*. UK ed., HarperCollins Publishers, 2012. https://amzn.to/31Re4Dc

7. when upside down will be turned right-side up

1. ---. "Priorities of Life—First Things First —." *Word-Strong with Trip Kimball*, 10 Aug. 2020, www.word-strong.com/home/priorities-of-life-first-things-first-rrme7.

8. contentment is a handful of peace and quiet

1. Roberts, Russell. "America and the World's Resources." *Foundation for Economic Education*, 1 Dec. 2001, fee.org/articles/america-and-the-worlds-resources.

2. "United States Population 2022 (Demographics, Maps, Graphs)." *Https://World-populationreview.Com/*, World Population Review, worldpopulationreview.com/ countries/united-states-population. Accessed 25 July 2022.

9. the cost of loneliness and great value of relationships

1. "The Preamble of the U.S. Constitution." *National Constitution Center – The Preamble of the U.S. Constitution*, constitutioncenter.org/interactive-constitution/ preamble. Accessed 23 Sept. 2021.

2. "United We Stand, Divided We Fall." *Wikiwand*, www.wikiwand.com/en/Unit ed_we_stand,_divided_we_fall. Accessed 23 Sept. 2021.

3. "Christians Struggled with Relational Health Prior to the Crisis—So What Has Changed?" *Barna Group*, www.barna.com/research/christians-relational-health. Accessed 23 Sept. 2021.

4. Charvat, Ph.D., Mylea. "The Impact of Social Isolation and Loneliness." *Psychology Today*, 29 May 2020, www.psychologytoday.com/us/blog/the-fifth-vital-sign/ 202005/the-impact-social-isolation-and-loneliness.

10. is change the only constant in life?

1. "Heraclitus." *Wikiwand*, www.wikiwand.com/en/Heraclitus. Accessed 23 Sept. 2021.
2. Kimball, Trip. "3 Approaches to Cultural Shifts - Publishous." *Medium*, 8 Mar. 2019, medium.com/publishous/3-approaches-to-cultural-shifts-14bcc8e84b63.

11. a better life with fewer words and much fewer promises

1. ---. "The Search to Know God —." *Word-Strong with Trip Kimball*, 9 July 2020, www.word-strong.com/blog/the-search-to-know-god-waxja.

12. when wealth is more of a problem than a blessing

1. "Second Industrial Revolution." *Wikiwand*, www.wikiwand.com/en/Second_Industrial_Revolution#/Socio-economic_impacts. Accessed 4 Oct. 2021.
2. "John D. Rockefeller - New World Encyclopedia." *New_World_Encyclopedia*, www.newworldencyclopedia.org/entry/John_D._Rockefeller. Accessed 4 Oct. 2021.
3. ---. "About Trip —." *Word-Strong with Trip Kimball*, www.word-strong.com/about. Accessed 4 Oct. 2021.

13. life's reward, god's gift, and a heart full of joy

1. "Life Is Beautiful | Official Trailer (HD) - Roberto Benigni, Nicoletta Braschi | MIRAMAX." *YouTube*, uploaded by https://www.youtube.com/c/miramax/about, 15 Jan. 2016, www.youtube.com/watch?v=8CTjcVr9Iao.

14. the deep dark pit of selfishness and self-pity

1. "Ecclesiastes 6 | NIV Bible | YouVersion." *YouVersion*, my.bible.com/bible/111/ECC.6.NIV. Accessed 5 Oct. 2021.

15. the frustrations and questions of an unsatisfied life

1. Kimball, Trip. "Most of the Rest of the World—MOTROW —." *Word-Strong with Trip Kimball*, 16 Jan. 2018, www.word-strong.com/thinking-out-loud/most-of-the-rest-of-the-world-motrow-c3xk4.
2. "Poverty Threshold." *Wikiwand*, www.wikiwand.com/en/Poverty_threshold. Accessed 5 Oct. 2021.

3. "First World Problem." *Wikiwand*, www.wikiwand.com/en/First_World_problem. Accessed 5 Oct. 2021.
4. ---. "Want to Know the Origin of FOMO? - Publishous." *Medium*, 23 July 2019, medium.com/publishous/want-to-know-the-origin-of-fomo-1b04340593d2.

16. a sober perspective based on inverted wisdom

1. "Conventional Wisdom." *The Merriam-Webster.Com Dictionary*, www.merriam-webster.com/dictionary/conventional%20wisdom. Accessed 5 Oct. 2021.
   "Prevailing Wisdom Definition | English Definition Dictionary | Reverso." *Https://Dictionary.Reverso.Net/*, dictionary.reverso.net/english-definition/prevailing+wisdom. Accessed 5 Oct. 2021,

17. wisdom to grasp a conundrum beyond our control

1. ---. "The Mystery of The Gospel: Unraveling God's Story —." *Word-Strong with Trip Kimball*, WestBow Press, 13 Sept. 2012, www.word-strong.com/shop/the-mystery-of-the-gospel-unraveling-gods-story-ly2a9.
2. "C.S. Lewis Shares 'Why I'm Not an Atheist.'" *YouTube*, uploaded by https://www.youtube.com/user/vernonjournal/about, 18 Aug. 2009, www.youtube.com/watch?v=DzaLp3aL_f8&feature=youtu.be.

18. schemes, snares, and the futility of personal goodness

1. Kimball, Trip. "A Blessed Longing and True Godliness —." *Word-Strong with Trip Kimball*, 29 July 2020, www.word-strong.com/home/a-blessed-longing-and-true-godliness-gxhfn.
2. Samples, Kenneth. "Imago Dei: What Does It Mean?" *Reasons to Believe*, 14 Apr. 2021, reasons.org/explore/publications/nrtb-e-zine/read/nrtb-e-zine/2011/08/01/imago-dei-what-does-it-mean.
3. Link, Julie Ackerman. "Nature Abhors a Vacuum." *Our Daily Bread*, 21 Jan. 2011, odb.org/US/2011/01/21/nature-abhors-a-vacuum.

20. enigmas, the fear of god, and a shadowy life

1. "Enigma Definition and Meaning | Collins English Dictionary." *Collins Dictionaries*, 7 Oct. 2021, www.collinsdictionary.com/us/dictionary/english/enigma.
2. "What Is the Law of Retribution?" *GotQuestions.Org*, 26 Apr. 2021, www.gotquestions.org/law-of-retribution.html.
3. "II Samuel 7:16 NKJV." *YouVersion*, www.bible.com/bible/114/2SA.7.16. Accessed 7 Oct. 2021.

4. "Lord Acton Quote | Online Library of Liberty." *Online Library of Liberty*, oll.liber tyfund.org/quotes/214. Accessed 7 Oct. 2021.
5. ---. "Rainbow Village Ministries —." *Word-Strong with Trip Kimball*, 1 Aug. 2016, www.word-strong.com/rainbow-village-ministries.

21. enjoying life is biblical and recommended

1. Johnson Ph.D., John A. "The Psychology of Expectations." *Psychology Today*, 17 Feb. 2018, www.psychologytoday.com/us/blog/cui-bono/201802/the-psychology-expectations.
2. Wikipedia contributors. "Epicureanism." *Wikipedia*, 10 Oct. 2021, en.wikipedia.org/wiki/Epicureanism.
3. ---. "The Relevance and Value of the Serenity Prayer - Publishous." *Medium*, 13 Feb. 2020, medium.com/publishous/the-relevance-and-value-of-the-serenity-prayer-94be44cb63cf.

22. the equality of death and hope for the living

1. Myburgh, Graeme. "Death Is the Great Equalizer (Quotes)." *Wisdom Trove*, 5 Aug. 2021, wisdomtrove.com/death-is-the-great-equalizer-quotes.
2. "Buddhism on the Afterlife." *ReligionFacts*, 17 Mar. 2015, religionfacts.com/buddhism/afterlife.
   Today, Hinduism. "Nine Beliefs of Hinduism." *Hinduism Today*, 1 July 2021, www.hinduismtoday.com/hindu-basics/nine-beliefs-of-hinduism.
3. "Harry Chapin - Cat's in the Cradle 1977." YouTube, uploaded by https://www.youtube.com/user/fritz51328/about, 23 Apr. 2015, www.youtube.com/watch?v=EUNZMiYo_4s.
   "Mac Davis -- Stop And Smell The Roses." *YouTube*, uploaded by https://www.youtube.com/channel/UCCg75ypkC66ecnF6B-9_Otg/about, 13 Nov. 2014, www.youtube.com/watch?v=oDfI6MrKNEc.

23. the power of commitment and the burden of potential

1. Schultz, Charles. "There Is No Heavier Burden." *Relics World Quotes*, 4 Nov. 2019, www.relicsworld.com/charles-m-schulz/there-is-no-heavier-burden-than-an-unful filled-potential-author.
2. Boehm, Rachel Nbc-Hwc. *Is There Truth to "Look Good, Feel Good"?* 17 Apr. 2022, www.linkedin.com/pulse/truth-look-good-feel-rachel-boehm-nbc-hwc.
   Also see– "The Psychology Behind the 'Look Good, Feel Good, Play Good' Philosophy." *USA Lacrosse Magazine*, www.usalaxmagazine.com/fuel/us-lacrosse/the-psychology-behind-the-look-good-feel-good-play-good-philosophy. Accessed 13 Sept. 2022.

24. wisdom is better than strength or weapons of war

1. Liew, Michelle B. "Top 10 Most Popular Personality Assessment Tests (and How You Can Benefit from Them)." *Learning Mind*, 31 Aug. 2020, www.learning-mind. com/personality-assessment-tests.

25. wisdom prepares the way for success

1. ---. "Medicine Show." *Wikipedia, 28 Sept. 2021, en.wikipedia.org/wiki/Medi cine_show.*
   Haynes, Andrew. "The History of Snake Oil." *The Pharmaceutical Journal*, 23 Jan. 2015, pharmaceutical-journal.com/article/opinion/the-history-of-snake-oil.
2. "Enron Scandal." *Wikiwand*, www.wikiwand.com/en/Enron_scandal. Accessed 16 Sept. 2022.
3. "Bernie Madoff: Who He Was, How His Ponzi Scheme Worked." *Investopedia*, 8 Sept. 2022, www.investopedia.com/terms/b/bernard-madoff.asp.
4. Kimball, Trip. "Do You Know What Leads to Communication Failure? - Publishous." *Medium*, 19 June 2020, medium.com/publishous/do-you-know-what-leads-to-communication-failure-6ab4b781ea6c.
5. MacKay, Jory. "Multitasking Is a Myth: The Ultimate Guide to Getting More Done (By Doing Less)." *RescueTime Blog*, 6 Aug. 2020, blog.rescuetime.com/multi tasking.

26. the vacuous and verbose nature of a fool

1. Wikipedia contributors. "Information Age." *Wikipedia*, 7 Oct. 2021, en.wikipedia. org/wiki/Information_Age.

27. the improbable certainty and mystery of faith

1. Staff, WeAreTeachers. "Lawnmower Parents Are the New Helicopter Parents and We Are Not Here for It." *We Are Teachers*, 6 Dec. 2018, www.weareteachers.com/ lawnmower-parents.
2. Plant, Renee. "What Is Tiger Parenting?" *Verywell Family*, 30 July 2021, www.very wellfamily.com/what-is-tiger-parenting-5188954.
3. Gauthier, Brandy. "Helicopter and Lawnmower Parents." *Brentwood Christian School*, 30 Nov. 2018, www.brentwoodchristian.org/blog/helicopter-and-lawn mower-parents.
4. "The Truman Show (1998) Trailer #1 | Movieclips Classic Trailers." *YouTube*, uploaded by https://www.youtube.com/c/MovieclipsCLASSICTRAILERS/about, 27 Feb. 2018, www.youtube.com/watch?v=dlnmQbPGuls.

28. the seductive appeal of youth and nostalgia

1. Smith, Brook. "Dodgers: Remembering Vin Scully's Most Memorable Dodgers Moments And Iconic Calls." *Dodgers Nation*, 3 Aug. 2022, www.dodgersnation.com/dodgers-remembering-vin-scullys-most-memorable-dodgers-moments-and-iconic-calls/2022/08/03.
2. Vanbuskirk, Sarah. "The Mental Health Benefits of Sunlight." *Verywell Mind*, 10 Dec. 2020, www.verywellmind.com/the-mental-health-benefits-of-sunlight-5089214.

29. remember your creator before your life slips into eternity

1. "GOD'S WORD Translation Bibles and Outreach Resources." *God's Word Mission Society*, godsword.org. Accessed 15 Oct. 2021.
2. "Evangelism Is Most Effective Among Kids." *Barna Group*, 11 Oct. 2004, www.barna.com/research/evangelism-is-most-effective-among-kids.

30. the hard truths of life, death, grief, and eternity

1. Holland, Kimberly. "What You Should Know About the Stages of Grief." *Healthline*, 25 Sept. 2018, www.healthline.com/health/stages-of-grief.
2. Friedman, Russell. "The Best Grief Definition You Will Find." *The Grief Recovery Method*, 4 June 2013, www.griefrecoverymethod.com/blog/2013/06/best-grief-definition-you-will-find.

epilogue

1. "What Is Christian Atheism?" *GotQuestions.Org*, 26 Apr. 2021, www.gotquestions.org/Christian-atheism.html.
2. Wikipedia contributors. "Christian Atheism." *Wikipedia*, 15 Oct. 2021, en.wikipedia.org/wiki/Christian_atheism.
3. Kimball, Trip. "Christianity Is Not About Moral Goodness - Publishous." *Medium*, 26 Mar. 2021, medium.com/publishous/christianity-is-not-about-moral-goodness-bc2e1b0d09bc.

acknowledgments

I'm thankful to those who've helped me with publishing this book! As always with any project, especially writing a book, there needs to be and ought to be an acknowledgment of others who contribute to it. This was a two-year project for me with lots of revisions and rewrites.

I'm thankful for my daughter Leanna's help in editing and for helping me rethink how to express and reorganize what I wanted to say. Also to Mackenzi Hill, who edited the final book draft after my many revisions.

I'm also thankful for the input, insight, and a bit of course correction for these devotional studies from my friends David Guzik, Lance Ralston, and Benjamin Sledge. Of course, this meant more revisions and rewriting, but that's where the real work of writing is done.

Thanks to Yab Techale and Will Potts for the initial design and layout of the cover. I'm picky about this stuff and they were a great help in bringing my thoughts and the content of the book to life on the cover. Thanks also to Leanna for her inspiration for the cover.

Daniel Williams, who formatted the cover of my previous book with his wife's artwork (Stories of Redemption), created the final cover design. The primary photo used in the background on the front is by Jeremy Bishop, and another by Austin Rich was used on the back cover. Daniel added some finishing touches and formatted the final layout.

Thanks also for the endorsements and feedback from my friends Bill Holdridge, Karl Vaters, Dan Finfrock, and Chapin Marsh! I'm also thankful to those who read my blog's original drafts and my postings on Medium. All of it was preparation for this book.

And, as always, I'm thankful for the Lord opening my eyes, mind, and heart to see and understand what He made known to me in writing these devotional studies!

If you enjoyed this book and believe it will be helpful to others, please leave a 5 star review on Amazon and share what you liked best.

Thanks!

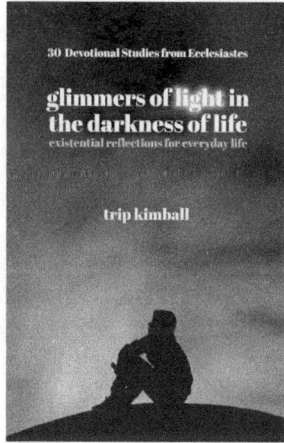

Reviews are helpful for better exposure online and on Amazon. Thanks!!!

Just scan the QR code and it will take you to the book on Amazon

about the author

I've had the privilege of planting a church in the US and establishing two ministries overseas, as well as many other ministry experiences.

I have a passion to disciple and mentor leaders and pastors within the US and overseas, and love to teach and train leaders whenever possible.

Writing has been a major part of what I do for the past several years. My writing projects include a book, training materials, and Bible studies for leaders and cross-cultural missions. I also post articles, devotionals, and Bible studies on my website– Word-Strong.com

I've served as a chaplain in a local restaurant and small business, and am one of several pastors serving with Poimen Ministries.

You can read more about Trip and see his weekly posts on his website — www.tripkimball.com

This is Trip's third published book.

f X ◎ a

also by trip kimball

— The Mystery of the Gospel (Revised and Updated Version) —
Unraveling God's Story of Redemption / the Essential Gospel

— Stories of Redemption —
A Devotional Journey Through the Book of Ruth

— Study Guide for the Book of Ruth —
A Living Word Study

— Study Guide for the Book of Ecclesiastes —
A Living Word Study

— An Introductory Guide to Inductive Bible Study —
a simple approach for studying the Bible

— Living Word Study Journal –
a companion for the study guide

———

These books are also available on the Shop page of my website–
https://tripkimball.com/shop
Also on my Amazon Author page — Trip Kimball
You can click on the QR code to go to my author page—

www.ingramcontent.com/pod-product-compliance
Lightning Source LLC
LaVergne TN
LVHW051401080426
835508LV00022B/2923